STUDY GUIDE

A Journey Through the Bible

Gordon Patterson

with Dorothy Dobson

A JOURNEY THROUGH THE BIBLE: STUDY GUIDE

Printed in Canada

ISBN: 978-1-77069-773-7

Word Alive Press
131 Cordite Road, Winnipeg, MB R3W 1S1
www.wordalivepress.ca

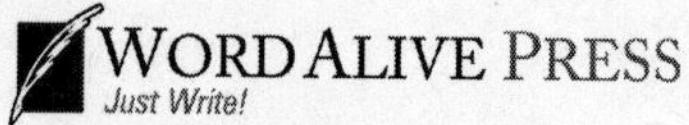

Cataloguing in Publication information may be obtained from Library and Archives Canada

INTRODUCTION

The questions and comments that follow are intended to be used as a companion booklet to *A Journey Through the Bible*. They are provided to stimulate personal reflection and can also be used to facilitate small group discussion. They are in no way meant to be a thorough study of the scriptures, but simply highlight specific Biblical passages with the intent of applying these truths in practical, everyday life.

Readers will be challenged to consider at a deeper level how their spiritual beliefs are lived out in their relationships, their use of time and abilities, and ultimately in their life's purpose and direction.

Reading through the entire Bible can seem to be a daunting pilgrimage. We believe the journey can be made easier and more rewarding by following the pattern laid out in the book and the study guide. We suggest you keep pen and journal handy so you can plot your progress by noting significant insights and personal decisions along the way.

May Christ's Spirit empower you and light the path ahead as you hear His voice.

—Rev. Gordon Patterson

THE BOOK OF *Genesis*

Chapters 1–3

1. Is there any circumstance or issue in your life for which you are blaming others? How can you take responsibility for your behaviours or attitudes?
2. What is it about human nature that makes forbidden fruit so desirable?

Chapters 4–6

1. Why do we find obedience to God so difficult?
2. Ask God to show you any bitterness or unfinished business you are reluctant to deal with in your life.

Chapters 7–9

1. Are you comfortable with the day-by-day focus and direction of your life? What may need to change?
2. Reflect on the important principles mentioned in the book by the author. Write down some specific goals and intentions you might set for yourself in the next month—or the next year.

Chapters 10–12

1. Do you believe God has a plan for your life?
2. What gets you off-track in your relationship with Jesus?
3. How do you see God's plan unfolding in present-day world events, particularly in Israel?

Chapters 13–15

1. Does your relationship with others reflect your relationship with God? What personal qualities and attitudes foster a growing closeness with others? With God?
2. What do you believe should be the response of the church, and you personally, to Jewish people and Israel?

Chapters 16–18

1. How do you explain the age-old conflict between Arabs and Jews?
2. How can God use our times of waiting and silence to help shape and mature us?
3. How can our relationship with fellow followers of Christ make a difference?

Chapters 19–21

1. Are you holding on to specific promises or personal revelations from God's Word? Will this help your personal growth?
2. How would you evaluate your daily Bible reading and meditation with God?
3. What might change or improve these disciplines?

Chapters 22–24

1. What is your response to the incredible test Abraham faced in being willing to sacrifice Isaac?
2. What do you think Isaac was feeling?
3. What particular challenge or test is God placing before you now? Your family? Others you know?
4. God clearly allowed Isaac the desire of his heart in granting Rebekah to become his wife. Recount an incident in your life where God directly answered your prayers in an awesome way.

Chapters 25–28

1. Chapters 26–27 are full of intrigue and deception. Have you ever been tempted to change or alter events by manipulation? What were the results?
2. What does the author suggest will help in dealing with disappointing realities and our negative responses?

Chapters 29–31

1. Chapter 29 describes how Laban used and tricked Jacob. Have you ever felt used and unappreciated by someone? If so, were you able to work through it to forgiveness? How?
2. The author states, "The real you is what you are like at home." Are there any attitudes, behaviours, or poor reactions you need to change towards those closest to you? If so, how can you do that?
3. The word "benediction" literally means "to speak good." How might you speak good words and encourage people in your life this week?

Chapters 32–35

1. Reflect upon what Jacob wrestling with God is all about. Have you ever wrestled with God? If so, what did you learn from it?
2. It appears that Jacob and Esau reconciled their relationship. How can one deal with relationships that seem to go sideways and stay that way?

Chapters 36–39

1. Reflect on the author's two dreams. How do you recognize the spiritual attacks from Satan? How have you learned to respond?
2. What lessons can be learned from the story of Joseph being sold into slavery? Do you sometimes feel that God is too harsh and unfair?

Chapters 40–41

1. Joseph suffered huge injustices and negative circumstances. How do you think he kept from being bitter and turning against God? What can we learn from this?
2. Blessing others and not cursing them is a key truth to be learned from Joseph's life. How can you put this into practice in your own life?
3. God sometimes uses dreams to give us understanding or direction. Do you have an example of that? How should we handle such dreams?

Chapters 42–46

1. From Joseph's example, how can we move from bitterness and unforgiveness to acceptance and forgiveness?
2. Spend some extended time in gratitude and praise to the Lord. How can thanksgiving and praise break down the walls of pain in our lives?

Chapters 47–50

1. In Chapter 49, Jacob blesses his sons. Why is it important to specifically honour and offer a blessing upon those closest to us? How might you go about this?
2. You may have been or are now experiencing an "Egypt" time in your life. What spiritual strategy might you use to help you through this seemingly hopeless time?

THE BOOK OF
Exodus

Chapters 1–3

1. Thinking back, what events and circumstances prepared you to be the person you are today? In what ways?
2. What are three of the most significant lessons you have learned from life?

Chapters 4–6

1. Is there a specific task or challenge God has placed before you for this time of your life? Seek the Lord in openness. It may not be obvious or for this season.
2. Are you possibly being called to be an Aaron—a person who supports and walks alongside another leader? If not, can you think of someone who is?

Chapters 7–10

1. Have you ever experienced setbacks as a result of being reluctant to do what you felt God was calling you to do?
2. What is God teaching you in this season of your life? Are there attitudes or choices He wants you to examine?

Chapters 11–13

1. Have you ever experienced or looked on and watched the Lord working through a tragedy or major upheaval in someone's life?
2. Have you ever confessed your sins to another person? Is there any person you truly trust or who can trust you with their deep personal story?

Chapters 14–15

1. Just as the Israelites quickly forgot God's miraculous deliverance, in what ways (past or present) have you slipped back into old patterns of belief and behaviour? How do you respond when you don't like the "you" inside your skin?
2. Why is it that praising God and being thankful can often be so difficult for us?

Chapters 16–18

1. How might you explain the "valley" times in life to a new believer, or to a child?
2. Why are so many of us reluctant to allow someone else to share our burdens or responsibilities?

Chapters 19–20

1. What habits or enemies of your soul do you struggle with? What needs to be done?
2. Reflect on the Ten Commandments (Exodus 20:3–10) and consider what each is saying to you about your relationship with Jesus Christ and with specific individuals who are part of your life.

Chapters 21–23

1. Life often seems to be too hard, too much to keep up with, too unrewarding. We know the rules, but we've lost the joy and the victory. In times like these, how can one keep from settling for "the glass half full" rather than the life that is promised by Jesus in John 10:10? What does the author suggest?

Chapters 24–27

1. Sometimes we feel that we have repeatedly broken faith with ourselves and in our promises to God. At times like these, what is important for us to remember? Write out some of God's promises to you.
2. What does the "priesthood of all believers" mean to you?

Chapters 28–31

1. What hinders us from taking "everything" before Jesus? Is it fear of losing approval? Shame? An unwillingness to change attitudes? Discouragement?
2. Think of a time when God has provided a clear answer to your prayer. Share it with others.

Chapters 32–34

1. Are there attitudes in our hearts or issues where we have, in effect, said to God, "Keep your hands off"?
2. Reflect on Exodus 34:6–7. This is a marvellous definition and description of our unchanging God! Write down ideas and thoughts that come to you as you meditate.

Chapters 35–37

1. Reflect or discuss what giving means to you—of your time? Your giftedness? Your money? Is it fulfilling to you?
2. Construction of the sanctuary was a team effort. In creating the Church, Jesus intended His Body to work and flow together for mutual benefit. If you were to describe a body part reflecting your place in the Body of Christ, what would it be? Why?

Chapters 38–40

1. Do you actively encourage and show appreciation for those around you and what they do? How can you do that today? Tomorrow?
2. Jesus says His followers are to be salt and light (Matthew 5:14). Ask the Lord to show you where you might consciously reflect His light in your daily routine today.

THE BOOK OF *Matthew*

Chapters 1–2

1. Most people would agree that Jesus, a humble and obscure carpenter, is the greatest and best known person in history. Why is it that so many fail to recognize Him as the Messiah?
2. Discuss these statements—People seldom truly encounter Jesus and remain neutral to Him. They are either drawn to Him or reject Him.

Chapter 3

1. Why are denying, covering up, or blaming others for our past hurts and failures the easiest paths to follow?
2. Repentance (turning around) is always difficult. Do you ever mentally bargain with God by offering good works or service as a substitute for making a decision to repent and face your failures?

Chapter 4

1. Everyone struggles with at least one besetting sin (wrong attitude). Can you name the area of struggle that you battle?
2. Share your responses to the three ways Jesus faced temptation listed by the author.

Chapter 5

1. Spend time reflecting on the powerful words of the Beatitudes (Matthew 5:5–12). What stands out or convicts you in these verses?

2. In Matthew 5:16–18, Jesus declares to you and me, "You *are* salt! You *are* light!" Do you have difficulty fully accepting the way God loves you? Do you respond with an attitude that says "I need to act like or try to become like salt and light" rather than choosing to accept the fact that you are already those things?
3. Meditate on Matthew 5:48. Write a prayer to the Lord expressing your responses to this amazing challenge. Share it with someone.

Chapter 6

1. For a few days, monitor the amount of time you actually spend in dialogue prayer (speaking and listening to God). What do you think about your findings?
2. Forgiveness is a choice. Regaining trust in a relationship may be a lengthy process. Why can waiting to "feel" like forgiving someone be a spiritual trap?
3. Reflect on Matthew 6:24. What competes for Jesus' full lordship in your life? Money? Success in the eyes of others? People pleasing?

Chapter 7

1. Reflect on these three verbs—ask, seek, knock. What do you passionately desire the Lord to grant you in your life? (See Psalm 37:4–7)
2. Reflect on the following statements: Our spiritual battle is a struggle within our minds. As we think and believe, so we live.

Chapters 8–9

1. Because of faulty doctrine and spiritual excess, many followers of Christ are uneasy and reluctant to pray for signs and wonders, such as physical healing. What might be a healthy and balanced approach to this kind of prayer? Is prayer for miraculous healing happening today in your worshipping community?

Chapters 10–11

1. Jesus sent out His disciples with the challenge to heal the sick, raise the dead, cleanse those who have leprosy, and drive out demons. Are these still His marching orders for us today? Why or why not? Where and how might this happen? How would you begin?

2. How might you, your family, or small group better create an atmosphere where others will experience the presence of Jesus? Give practical suggestions.
3. What do Jesus' words in Matthew 11:30 actually mean to you? *"For my yoke is easy and my burden is light."*

Chapter 12

1. What thinking or behaviour patterns do you see in yourself that are reminiscent of the Pharisees?
2. Often the very things we complain about or criticize in others are our own shortcomings and weaknesses (Matthew 12:34). Do you agree? Why or why not?

Chapter 13

1. After reading the parable of the sower, are you prepared to be available with all that you have and are, to be used by the Lord? How can you be open and ready to share your life on a daily basis?
2. Like any crop, our lives of faith in Christ are in an ongoing state of change, whether we're either growing and maturing, or wilting and dying. Is your spiritual life maturing or wasting away? Reflect on the three areas the author suggests that prevent a harvest.

Chapter 14

1. John the Baptist's life ended so tragically. How do you respond to the "why" questions in life, where events and circumstances seem to make no sense? How can you help someone who is struggling with bitterness and anger at God?
2. Like walking on water, has God placed a vision or challenge before you that seems far too big, too much to ask or expect? Share your vision with someone.

Chapters 15–16

1. Most of us don't completely live out what we say and believe. Are there areas in your life where your words and actions conflict? What are you prepared to do about it?

Chapters 17–18

1. Like Peter, we so often want to do something for God apart from just dwelling in His presence. Are you, perhaps unwittingly, robbing yourself of Christ's fullness of grace and truth by being too busy?
2. Reflect on the characteristics of a child. What childlike qualities might you need to develop in your walk of faith?

Chapters 19–20

1. The rich young man was like many of us today: he wanted to do the right thing but was divided within himself. Some of the "gods" of our culture—time, money, things—crowd out Jesus' lordship in our life. What might be getting you off-track in your spiritual life?
2. If Jesus were to ask what you want Him to do for you, do you really know or want all He might be prepared to give you? Being healed brings major new responsibilities and life changes!

Chapters 21–22

1. Reflect on Matthew 22:37–38 and ask yourself what each clause means to you in a specific way.
2. Love is far more than a thought or positive feeling. How do you truly bless, build up, and encourage the "neighbours" in your life, especially those who are difficult to love?

Chapters 23–25

1. Our desire for the approval of others can often obscure and drown out God's voice and direction in our lives. Think about examples of this in your own life.
2. Being available and ready to do what God asks of us is an inner skill and discipline to be developed. Would you agree? How often do you check in with God and make yourself available to Him?

Chapters 26–28

1. When have you slept—or run off in fear, or become distracted by life—and missed the significance of what God is asking of us?
2. When was the last time you truly confessed your sins?
3. Reflect upon and/or share with someone the experience and blessing of being forgiven by Jesus—the peace, the joy, the renewed hope!

THE BOOK OF *Leviticus*

Chapters 1–7

1. The author speaks of the lifetime commitment needed in order to seek to know God. Can you identify areas of deepening faith and growth in your relationship with Jesus over the past year? Do you have goals for the year ahead?
2. Spend some time asking the Lord to reveal areas of hidden sin, such as circumstances or relationships. What is the next step?

Chapters 8–12

1. Have you ever been anointed with oil or used oil in praying for others? Has it been helpful? How?
2. What is your understanding of manifestations of the Holy Spirit within yourself or others? Do you have areas of confusion or unbelief?

Chapters 13–17

1. What might be considered the "leprosy" of our culture today? What is society doing about it? What do you think God's attitude might be?
2. Reflect on the two necessary ingredients suggested by the author for living the Christian life. Write down your thoughts or ideas.

Chapters 18–22

1. Think back over your conversations of the past few days. Did your words build up and encourage others? Were they always true?

2. Reflect on your inner life and ask yourself the following questions: Is my life too self-absorbed? Are there areas of self-pity or defeat? Would I choose to do anything differently?

Chapters 23–25

1. Do you take regular time to relax, unwind, and slow down? How do you do this?
2. Do you know of any church or Christian group that celebrates the four Jewish festivals described by the author? Do you think it is important for Christians and Jews to foster closer ties and friendship with one another? Why?

Chapters 26–27

1. We are quick to enjoy and respond to the blessings in our lives, but what about God's judgment of our culture? As we look at what is happening in our western culture, is this the natural result of putting material gain, personal comfort, and selfish goals ahead of the worship of God?

THE BOOK OF *Numbers*

Chapters 1–4

1. Praising God is not necessarily an inborn quality that comes without conscious effort. Like learning to play a musical instrument or a sport, skill is developed through ongoing effort and practice. This being so, how might you need to change your worship habits?
2. When we are in His will, He shows us how to be organized in our planning. What changes do you think God would like to make in the way you go about your daily living?

Chapters 5–9

1. The familiar blessing of Numbers 6:24–26 is a promise God makes to every one of us as His followers. Claim each part of it for yourself in a specific way.
2. Look back at your life and pick out places you feel God has guided your way.

Chapters 10–12

1. Take time to think about the three lessons suggested in this passage and write down how they apply to your life.

Chapters 13–17

1. Attitude is everything! Ask the Lord to show you the attitude you need to have in every circumstance you are facing right now. This will take time and conscious effort!

2. In what parts of your life do you become your own worst enemy by your anxieties and problems? How can you trust God to help you change that attitude?

Chapters 18–21

1. Asking God to give us a grateful, thankful heart for the daily load we carry is a discipline to be learned. It is not easy. It takes a lifetime, but it starts with a choice and a decision. The positive emotions follow!
2. It is good to have someone in your life to whom you can open up your heart—and it is good to be that someone for a friend. Pride, fear and unwillingness to be accountable can keep us in a place of negative habits and attitudes.

Chapters 22–24

1. Israel is clearly a unique people group and nation on the world scene. Why is it that almost the whole world is against them? Is there a spiritual connection to the animosity so many nations direct towards Israel? Consider Numbers 24:9.
2. Are you connected with other followers of Christ on a regular basis? If not, why? Do you specifically pray that those in leadership may be blessed and encouraged? Why might this be important?

Chapters 25–29

1. Think about your circle of friends. Who do you think God has given to you to pray for?
2. Almost nobody enjoys or welcomes confrontation. Think of an occasion where it might be right to speak out openly when someone is exhibiting bad behaviour or making wrong choices.

Chapters 30–36

1. Reflect on Numbers 30:2. Are you a person of your word, of integrity? The word "integrity" is derived from the words integrate and renew, meaning to bring parts together as a whole. To what degree are our words, beliefs, and actions integrated?
2. Are you accountable to someone in your life regarding setting goals and being honest about areas of struggle and vulnerability? If your answer is no, is this an excuse?

THE BOOK OF *Mark*

Chapter 1

1. Read Mark 1:35. Do you spend time regularly meeting with God alone, without distractions and interruptions?

Chapters 2–3

1. Read Mark 2:1–5 and consider the faith, compassion, and persistence of the four men who brought the paralytic to Jesus. When have you had that boldness?
2. Read Mark 3:34–35. Do you have a sense of "family" intimacy with a group you belong to? What hinders that kind of closeness in our daily life?

Chapters 4–5

1. Reflect on the parable of the sower and the seed. How might each type of soil reflect your response to God's Word? What is the Holy Spirit teaching you from this story?
2. Read Mark 5:1–20, and take particular note of verse 17. What would your response have been if you had been there?

Chapters 6–7

1. Read Mark 6:12–13. Have you ever openly shared the gospel message? Why do you think that doing so is a rare idea for many of Jesus' followers today?
2. Jesus shares some very strong words with the Pharisees and teachers of the law (Mark 6:5–13). How might these same words apply to the

Church in our culture today? How can we translate this teaching into practical, realistic action?

Chapters 8–9

1. Regarding the feeding of the four thousand people in Mark 8, the author suggests four steps she follows in dealing with problems. Using the same steps, take something you are currently facing to God. He longs to be involved in our circumstances.
2. Reflect on the incredible story in Luke 9:14–29. God always wants honesty from us, yet often we do not seek to expand our depth of faith in God. How might we, like the boy's father, move toward the cry of his heart, which is "Help me overcome my unbelief"?

Chapters 10–11

1. Mark 10:1 refers to Jesus' custom of teaching wherever He went. How do you represent Jesus in your daily life?
2. Many sobering statements arise from the interaction between Jesus and the rich young man. Write down the questions and emotions that arise within you from this passage. Share them with a friend and then seek the Lord's direction.

Chapters 12–13

1. Does the amount of our giving reflect the commitment we are making of our lives? How do you respond to that?
2. Tithing is nowhere mentioned in the New Testament. Why do you think that is so?

Chapters 14–16

1. What is your response to the story in Mark 14:3–9? How might this action be translated in our day?
2. Each of us, as followers of Jesus, has betrayed our best intentions to do the right thing. What can we learn from this kind of failure?
3. The author summarizes the ways in which Jesus prepared Himself to face the cross. How would you commit yourself to following through these steps in a situation you are presently facing?

THE BOOK OF *Deuteronomy*

Chapters 1–3

1. As they reached the border of the Promised Land, the Israelites were overcome with fear. What are the fears that block you from moving ahead in your life?
2. We all have wilderness experiences in our lives. How would you respond to someone who is passing through this kind of time?

Chapters 4–5

1. Do you ever deny, excuse, or ignore being obedient to what you know is right?
2. Do you agree that being a channel for God's love to reach others is really the only purpose worth living for?
3. We are challenged in these chapters to seek God first and always (Deuteronomy 4:29). Are you doing this in a daily, disciplined way? How could you improve in this?

Chapters 6–7

1. Self-centred attitudes, like self-pity, can cut us off from intimacy and joy in our walk with Christ. How do you deal with that problem?
2. Reflect on Deuteronomy 7:6. Do you feel highly valued by God? If not, why?

Chapters 8–9

1. What do you think God expects of you in your daily life? Do you enjoy life with God?

2. Take some time to list the blessings God is pouring into your life right now.

Chapters 10–12

1. Do you agree that people who pray are the power centre for the world?
2. How can we love the Lord our God with all our heart, soul, and strength (Deuteronomy 6:4)?

Chapters 13–15

1. Worry and anxiety can be very draining. What advice would you give someone who is dealing with anxious thoughts?
2. Giving generously of all we possess is a basic expectation in both the Old and New Testaments. What does it mean to you to be a good steward of your time, energy, and money?

Chapters 16–18

1. How could you make your celebrations at Christmas, Easter, and Thanksgiving more meaningful?
2. Do you think it would be helpful for us to observe some of the Biblical Jewish feasts? Jesus celebrated them.

Chapters 19–27

1. Taking the Promised Land was a huge challenge. Do you have a dream or goal that has never been fulfilled? What can you do about it?
2. Are there idols in your life (such as the golden calf for the Israelites) like busyness, materialism, or reputation that distract you?

Chapters 28–31

1. As good parents model character to their children, how can you model the love and truth of Jesus to those who are part of your daily life?
2. Reflect on this statement: "He accepts and encourages me so that I can accept and encourage others."
3. Meditate on Deuteronomy 30:19–20. What choices do you need to make right now?

Chapters 32–34

1. Reflect on Deuteronomy 33:27. Do you truly feel safe with God?

2. Just as Moses prayed a blessing over each tribe as they entered the Promised Land, write down a prayer of blessing you would like to give a significant person in your life.

THE BOOK OF *Joshua*

Chapters 1–4

1. In Joshua 1:5, we are given an incredible promise of God—to Joshua, but it's also for all of us as believers: *"I will never leave you nor forsake you."* Begin to make a list of God's promises from Scripture which have been personally meaningful to you.
2. Joshua 1:6–7 makes it clear that our part in God's promises is dependent on us closely walking out His commandments and obeying His law. Consider some ways that one can easily get off-track in following Jesus.
3. Think about a time when the Father prepared the way for you by providing a "Rahab" person or circumstance.

Chapters 5–8

1. Joshua 5:13–6:27 records the amazing story of the fall of Jericho. God's plans and how He thinks are so different from ours. Share a time when God has set up an event or experience utterly beyond your planning or reasoning.
2. Joshua 7 deals with the disobedience and sin of Achan. Consider how the sin of one person or a small number can negatively impact a family, community, or congregation. What is to be learned here?

Chapters 9–12

1. Making choices apart from Godly counsel and not personally waiting for the Holy Spirit's leading can wreak havoc in our lives. Do you consistently "wait" for God's leading in the management of your life?

2. Are you accountable to anyone for your life choices and lifestyle? Why is it important to have accountability prayer partners?
3. Think about a time when God worked through a seemingly impossible obstacle or situation to teach you that He is continually with you.

Chapters 13–16

1. As Joshua and the Israelites obeyed God's plans, they prospered. Why is it that letting go of our desires and plans is so difficult?
2. Has fear of failure and self-interest ever kept you from experiencing God's best plans for you?
3. Reread about Caleb in Joshua 14:6–15. His name means "faithful." What qualities did he possess that we should covet for ourselves? Why?

Chapters 17–21

1. God's plans and promises for Israel were being fulfilled, but the process was slow. Why is waiting for God's way often so difficult for us?
2. Do you have a clear sense of God's purpose for your life? For this season of life?
3. Consider and share how a small thing—such as a word of encouragement, a kind action from someone—has had a significant impact on your life. What can you do for someone else today that could impact his or her life?

Chapters 22–24

1. Reflect upon Joshua 23:14–16. The simple spiritual truth here is that we reap what we sow (Galatians 6:7). What lessons are you learning about sowing and reaping in your faith walk?
2. Our lives are woven together by the choices we make. Reflect on Joshua 24:15–16. What might it mean for you to choose God's way and serve Him faithfully today? And in the future?

THE BOOK OF *Luke*

Chapter 1

1. Reflect on the fact that throughout history God invariably uses ordinary people like Mary and Elizabeth to be part of amazing things in His Kingdom. What examples come to mind?
2. Mary's complete acceptance of God's plans for her is truly remarkable. Have you ever said "No way!" to God's leading in your life?

Chapter 2

1. In the incredible series of stories revolving around the birth of Jesus, what intrigues you most?
2. What can we learn from the fact that Jesus was thirty years old before the Father released Him to the fullness of His ministry?

Chapters 3–4

1. John preached a message of repentance. Why is repentance so essential for full salvation in Jesus?
2. What temptations do you face in daily living? How did Jesus respond to temptation?
3. Luke 4:18–19 (the fulfillment of Isaiah 61:1–2) provides Jesus' job description. How might each of these redemptive aspects of Jesus' ministry (preaching the good news, proclaiming freedom, etc.) be applied to your life?

Chapters 5–6

1. What is to be learned by Simon Peter's flexibility and obedience in Luke 5:5?
2. Reflect and discuss the author's four insights regarding our sense of unworthiness when we truly meet Christ.
3. Along with obedience to God, what other pillars are essential for our faith to be established upon rock, not sand?

Chapters 7–8

1. What do you believe about the power of physical healing by Jesus Christ? What questions still remain?
2. Salvation in Jesus is the ultimate "healing," and God says yes to every sincere cry for forgiveness and renewal in Him. How are salvation and healing connected?

Chapters 9–10

1. How would you explain to a child the concept of taking up your cross daily? (Luke 9:23)
2. What are some clear spiritual lessons to be learned from the parable of the Good Samaritan? (Luke 10:25–38)
3. Is there an attitude in your life today that needs Jesus' attention?

Chapter 11

1. Why is it important to be persistent in prayer, to keep on asking? Seeking? Knocking?
2. What are you doing to embrace and receive *all* of what God wants to give you?

Chapter 12

1. None of us fully live up to what we believe and what we would like to be. How do we keep from being hypocrites?
2. There is a personal cost to being a follower of Jesus. What in your life needs to be given over to Jesus?
3. What do you treasure most in your life?

Chapters 13–14

1. *"For the love of money is a root of all kinds of evil"* (1 Timothy 6:10). How can money and possessions become a god that keeps Jesus from truly being the Lord of our lives?
2. How can one live in our culture and determine what is a "need" and what is a "want"?

Chapters 15–16

1. What guidelines for living would you suggest to keep a follower of Jesus morally clean and upright, yet not legalistic?
2. Do you identify with the prodigal son or with the older brother? How does one combat self-centredness?
3. In what areas of life can we easily become double-minded? Where is your point of greatest weakness?

Chapters 17–18

1. Which aspect of yourself do you least admire?
2. How can a believer know when God is saying "Yes," "No," or "Wait"?
3. What does it mean to see our issues and problems "through the eyes of Jesus"?

Chapter 19

1. Open confession of sin and lifestyle changes brought transforming salvation to Zaccheus. What do you believe about confessing your sins to others? (James 5:16)
2. What lessons are to be learned from the parable of the ten minas in terms of how we invest all of ourselves to God's Kingdom?

Chapters 20–21

1. In what ways do you see Satan undermining the building of Christ's Kingdom in the North American Church and in our culture today? How should we respond and pray?
2. Reflect on the incredible re-creation of the state of Israel in 1948 and all that has followed since then. Is God saying something to His Church today regarding Israel?

Chapters 22–24

1. Just as God has a perfect plan in mind for each of His children, so has Satan: to keep us from intimacy and obedience to Jesus. In what way does Satan deceive you? How about the Church?
2. Have you, like Pilate, ever walked away from a situation that was unjust rather than get involved? How would you respond to a similar challenge?
3. Jesus' outstretched arms of love, acceptance, and forgiveness are always open to receive us. Pray for a deeper passion and Christ-likeness in your life, and ask the Lord to show you what that looks like.

THE BOOK OF *Judges*

Chapters 1–3

1. Do you believe God has a plan for your life? If so, what is it right now?
2. In our spiritual journey, all of us can be careless in following God's guidance. What consequences have you faced because of your rebellion? Have you grown personally as a result?

Chapters 4–6

1. Like Gideon, when we face tragedy and chaos we sometimes ask God, "Why?" But why do you think people rarely ask the Lord to explain all the goodness, love, and beauty He has showered on them?
2. What are the positive and negative aspects of putting a "fleece test" before God?

Chapters 7–10

1. God used Gideon's small army of three hundred to defeat an immense army. How has God used small everyday things to bring a significant change in your life or someone else's?
2. The Israelites repeatedly turned away from the Lord and worshipped false gods. We, too, as followers of Jesus, have a pattern of disobedience—sin/confess, sin/confess. In what ways can we break this cycle and discover wholeness?
3. In our country and culture, we appear to be increasingly turning our backs on God. Pray for our government leaders and for the Church to bring a return to biblical truths and faith in Jesus to our land.

Chapters 11–13

1. Many of us react negatively in self-centred and resentful ways. How can these impulses be reversed?
2. Reflect on the two points the author makes regarding serving others. What specifically do you need to change in your attitude?
3. How has the Lord brought you back on-track when you have failed Him or "blown it"?

Chapters 14–16

1. Name two or three spiritual truths to be learned from the story of Samson.
2. Just as God chose Samson for a special task, what specific assignment might God have for you in this season of your life?

Chapters 17–21

1. The repeated refrain *"everyone did as they saw fit"* (Judges 21:25) reflects clearly the mood of our culture, and even the Church today. How strong and real is your commitment to Jesus Christ? To His Church?
2. The creation of the nation of Israel in 1948 after being non-existent for almost nineteen centuries is a modern-day miracle. What do you believe and what does the Scripture say about what God is doing in our times?

THE BOOK OF *Ruth*

1. Ruth and Naomi model an inspiring relationship between the generations. Is there someone in your life of a different generation with whom you are consciously seeking to learn from or mentor?
2. Ruth was a foreigner and outsider. Are we consciously aware of the people who are foreigners among us? How can we improve our welcome to these people?

THE BOOK OF *John*

Chapter 1

1. Getting to know Christ, like any friendship, is made up of many decisions, large and small. Are you getting into a closer relationship with Jesus? Is your faith a living reality or mostly a set of beliefs?
2. Many ask, "Who is God?" He is like Jesus. Jesus gives a face to God. Who is Jesus to you?

Chapters 2–3

1. Turning the water into wine was not a world-changing miracle, but it reveals God's concern for us in the daily events of life. How have you experienced His answer to your needs?
2. How would you explain John 3:3 to a ten-year-old?

Chapter 4

1. Reflect back on special times of spiritual encounters with Jesus. If you are not sure of whether or not you have encountered Him, invite Him to meet with you now!
2. Reflect on Jesus' all-embracing love for every person—regardless of their race, their age, or their past.

Chapters 5–6

1. In spite of much evidence, the religious leaders of Jesus' day could not see Him for who He truly was. Where do you see that happening today?

2. Take a few quiet moments to ask the Holy Spirit to bring to your mind people and/or circumstances for which you have negative judgments or unforgiveness.
3. In the story of the feeding of the five thousand, the boy gave up his lunch. What is the lesson here for us?

Chapters 7–8

1. Your body must have food, water, and rest every day in order to function. In your spiritual life, how can you be more teachable, willing to learn and change in your walk of faith with God?

Chapters 9–10

1. In light of Jesus healing the blind man, ask the Holy Spirit where there may be areas of spiritual, relational, and emotional blindness in your life.
2. Reflect on the powerful word pictures the author describes in Jesus being a gate and the good shepherd for the sheep. Why is it important to see yourself as a sheep that is vulnerable, dependent, and needy without a shepherd?

Chapter 11

1. What is it that keeps many of us from calling out to our friends, and to God, when we face difficulties?
2. Reflect on the five points the author makes in the process involved in the raising of Lazarus from death. In what ways can you let Jesus and others close to you into your sphere of darkness, pain, and need?

Chapters 12–13

1. Like Mary, are you willing sometimes to be extravagant in your giving and sharing with others? How have you done that recently?
2. Do busyness and distractions keep you from deeper intimacy with God? If so, what can you do about it?
3. What is our culture's equivalent of "washing feet"? How would it translate in your personal life?

Chapters 14–15

1. Reflect on ways you have experienced the peace of Christ in the midst of confusion and anxiety (John 14:27).

2. Consider how Jesus is or is not the Way (direction), the Truth (wisdom and understanding), and the Life (purpose) in your faith journey (John 14:6).
3. Jesus' repeated command in John 15 is that we love one another. Then He tells us three times that He wants us to bear fruit—fruit that will last. Are changes necessary in your life for you to abide in Jesus, to love others, and to bear fruit?

Chapters 16–17

1. Reflect on the three ways the author describes the Holy Spirit being active in our lives.
2. Take time to pray specifically into the four areas the author suggests for people in your circle of concern.
3. Name individuals you believe the Lord has given you to pray for, encourage, and bless. Allow the Holy Spirit to guide you in prayer and actions with these people.

Chapters 18–19

1. Peter denied knowing Jesus to avoid trouble with the religious authorities. How do you think you would respond if being a Christian brought you persecution?
2. Pilate, like Peter, caved in to crowd pressure. How can we, as Christians, prepare to stand alone against the influence of the crowd?

Chapters 20–21

1. Every follower of Jesus is called to be a full-time Christian witness—no exceptions! How do you personally respond to the mission Christ is asking you to fulfill?
2. In reaffirming Peter's loyalty, Jesus makes it clear that the test of our commitment is how we treat others. Reflect on how you measure up.

THE BOOK OF
1 Samuel

Chapters 1–3

1. Virtually every one of us faces a "giant" in our lives—a besetting sin, a life circumstance, etc. It seems too much, too big for us to deal with. What can we learn from Hannah?
2. What experience have you had of hearing God's voice speak to you?

Chapters 4–6

1. As God's presence was often evident to the Israelites, do you sense His presence in our culture today? Why do you think that is?
2. How can you bring God's presence into our midst?

Chapters 7–8

1. What do you think is the value of fasting and personal times of silence?
2. Have you ever put too much confidence in someone to "save" you rather than in Jesus Christ? What did you learn from the experience?

Chapters 9–12

1. Saul was a specially anointed leader of his people. Do you believe there is a specific call for all followers of Jesus? How can one know this?
2. Gratitude is what brings us into His presence, and that is where we get our direction. Discuss.

Chapters 13–15

1. Have you, like Saul, impatiently moved ahead of God in seeking to solve an issue in your life? What were the results?
2. Reflect on 1 Samuel 15:23: *"For rebellion [disobedience, resentment, and negative criticism] is like the sin of divination [witchcraft], and arrogance like the evil of idolatry."*

Chapters 16–18

1. Reflect on the seven qualities mentioned by the author that describe David's character and also qualify him to be king. What specifically speaks to you?
2. David was a courageous man whose full confidence was in God. How can we deepen our faith walk to become more like David?

Chapters 19–24

1. Saul was overwhelmed by jealousy of David, insecurity, and fear. How can we avoid allowing these emotions to rob and potentially destroy our relationships with others and with God?
2. We all are influenced by others, positively and negatively. How can we maintain a healthy balance of dependence and independence in our relationships?

Chapters 25–31

1. In our increasingly sensual and morally-relative culture, what can best help build strong, long-lasting marriages? What can we and the church do in this regard?
2. Starting out with such great promise, Saul's life ultimately ended as a tragic, broken failure. What lessons can we learn from his life?

THE BOOK OF
2 Samuel

Chapters 1–5

1. All of us long for the closeness and security of a friendship like the one David and Jonathan shared. What qualities do you need in someone with whom you could be fully transparent and safe? Are you that kind of a friend to someone else?
2. What personal qualities did David possess that made him a great leader and king?
3. Each of us has "clay feet," or besetting sin. For David, it was making bad choices in his relationships with women. What is your area of weakness? How are you dealing with it?

Chapters 6–10

1. How would you describe your worship life—both private and in corporate settings? Is it free, open, and growing, or is it forced and mechanical? What would improve your worship?
2. Reflect on 2 Samuel 6:20. How do you consciously bless those who are closest to you? Do they feel blessed by you? How might you change things?

Chapters 11–15

1. In what ways do we gloss over our sinful attitudes and justify, or even deny, our bad behaviour?
2. Sin in our lives always brings a form of destruction, whether it be emotional, spiritual, or relational. How might unacknowledged sin in

your life cause suffering and separation between you and someone you love?

3. In 2 Samuel 15, we see David fully owning and repenting of his sin. Have you ever confessed your sin before the Lord? How did that make you feel?

Chapters 16–19

1. Turning the other cheek (Matthew 5:39) and not retaliating when insulted or attacked is one of the most difficult challenges we face in our Christian walk. Why is that?
2. Loving God and loving each other (Matthew 22:37–40) is the very core of the life of faith in Christ. Why do we often make this so difficult and complicated?

Chapters 20–24

1. Consider and discuss the author's comments regarding Israel and the Jewish people.
2. Reflect upon the spiritual truths in 2 Samuel 22:1–4. Do you call out to the Lord when your life becomes overwhelming and fearful? What have you discovered about God at such times?
3. What does it mean for you today to give your whole life to God as a living sacrifice? (Romans 12:1)

THE BOOK OF
Acts

Chapters 1–2

1. Do you ever experience the undeniable power of the Holy Spirit in your life? Do you ask and seek His power? If not, who do you think would pray with you to receive the Holy Spirit?
2. Reflect on Acts 1:7–8, 38. How do you explain or define the baptism or the fullness of the Holy Spirit?

Chapters 3–5

1. Reflect on Acts 3:19. Is there sin anywhere in your life that is ignored, repressed, or passively accepted? What can you do about it?
2. What one thing are you prepared to do to declare God's truth and love? Within your circle of family and friends? Your church? Your community?
3. In your personal prayer life, do you pray with great expectation for God's signs and wonders to be evident?

Chapters 6–7

1. Do you believe in the power and need for prayer to undergird our homes, congregations, and communities. Is it truly happening in your life? Your church?
2. Following Stephen's magnificent example (Acts 7:60), are you prepared to forgive your enemies? What enemies do you have? Fear? Anger? Self-pity? Discuss with someone ways you can forgive them.

Chapters 8–9

1. Think about Acts 8:4. How often do you actually speak about the Lord and spiritual issues in the course of your day? With whom do you speak?
2. Reflect on Acts 8:20–23. Because Satan is a deceiver, we can sometimes be blinded to sinful attitudes and emotions in our lives. Ask the Lord to show you what He sees in you.
3. Have you ever had a divine encounter where God seems to orchestrate a time, place, and people coming together, as in the story of Philip and the Ethiopian? Have you ever missed the opportunity in such a situation?

Chapters 10–11

1. Reflect upon times when you have experienced a oneness of heart and mind with a stranger who was a fellow believer.
2. What are some of the most interesting/difficult sociocultural barriers to cross with other nationalities in your community?

Chapters 12–13

1. Persecution and judgmental attitudes towards those who are different seem to be part of fallen humanity. What people groups or kinds of people do you struggle with in your city or community? Ask the Lord if there is anything you should do about it.
2. What ways has God used to adjust your prideful attitudes and bring awareness of your sin?

Chapters 14–15

1. Do you truly want *all* of the Holy Spirit's power and gifting that God wants to give you? Are there areas of confusion and uneasiness about the work and ministry of the Holy Spirit? How might you best resolve this?
2. What is the principal truth reflected in Acts 15:28–29? How do you determine when a practice or attitude is scriptural truth and when it is really cultural and legalistic?
3. How can bitterness and unforgiveness become like a cancer in relationships? What is the answer?

Chapters 16–17

1. God clearly showed Paul that he was to go to Macedonia. Has God placed a call on your life? If so, are you following it?
2. Our culture tends to encourage us to live out of our emotions. For example, we say, "If it feels good, do it." Like Paul and Silas singing praises in jail, how does Christ's peace and joy transcend even the worst circumstances?

Chapters 18–19

1. As you read Acts 18, ask yourself, "What is the condition of my heart towards God?" (Perhaps it's soft, stony, open, warm, etc.)
2. Why do we see/hear so little about miracles of healing today?
3. Acts 19 describes ongoing opposition to Paul's ministry. Where do you see the spiritual warfare that is going on within you? Your church? Your country?

Chapters 20–23

1. Paul experienced ongoing persecution and hardship. How does our easy-going religious freedom diminish our effectiveness and depth of commitment to serving Christ?
2. Reflect on Acts 20:24. Are you able to make this your testimony? If not, how do you need to change?

Chapters 24–26

1. The author speaks about the power of our words to build up or damage others. Do your daily conversations generally encourage and bless others, or do they put down and wound them? Consider some of your recent conversations in this light.
2. If you are a Christ follower, how do you think you are viewed by those who know you best in your community, in your workplace, and by your fellow believers? Does your life reflect Jesus?

Chapters 27–28

1. Though his life was continually threatened, Paul never questioned that he was going to go to Rome. Do you have the same determination and willingness to put effort into God's assignment for you? What do you think God's direction for you is?

2. From the time of his conversion, Paul maintained an ongoing dialogue with God through prayer (Acts 27:23–26). Are you a good listener when you talk to God?

THE BOOK OF
1 Kings

Chapters 1–3

1. Jealousy, perceived hurt, and harsh words can often undermine and destroy closeness in families. Think about each of your family members. Are there any with whom you struggle? Ask God to show you what part you can play in reconciling that relationship.
2. Reflect on Solomon's prayer in 1 Kings 3:9. What is so powerful about it?

Chapters 4–6

1. Initially Saul obeyed God at every point in his life. Why is obedience to God so crucial in our spiritual walk? What happens when we cut corners and ignore His precepts and guidance?
2. Spending adequate, quality time with our Lord is essential if we are to keep on-track spiritually. What steps can we take to assure that our time with Jesus is not just an "add-on" but a daily priority?

Chapters 7–9

1. Like Solomon, it is so easy to drift into patterns of behaviour and attitudes contrary to God's best for us. In what ways can Satan draw us away from a close, passionate intimacy with God?
2. Do you have someone in your life to whom you are spiritually accountable? Someone who can ask you the hard questions? Why is this important? Do you think it is really necessary?

Chapters 10–12

1. Solomon was known for his wisdom. How does one become a wise person? What inner qualities do you ask the Lord to give you?
2. Riches and power can blind us to God and His plan for us. What areas of your life might be spiritual blind spots—things that you neglect, deny, or excuse?
3. Are you open to facing God directly with who you are and allowing Him to change your heart, your mind, and your actions that are displeasing to Him? What changes do you think He might want right now?

Chapters 13–15

1. How do we know when we have heard from the Lord? How can we recognize when God is using another person to speak into our lives?
2. Often, like Rehoboam, we are people pleasers wanting others' approval rather than following what we know is God's will for us. How can we overcome our "fear of men"?
3. Take some time to specifically pray for the government leaders and those in authority over us.

Chapters 16–18

1. Sometimes the Lord places us in situations—at home, at work, in the community—where we witness injustice and destructive or cruel behaviour. Are there any real life situations where God might be calling you to stand up and speak out?
2. Our passivity and silence can become a vote for the enemy. How might we, as followers of Jesus, combat the destructive practices within our community and be a positive influence for righteous living?

Chapters 19–22

1. How can you get to that place of true inner quietness, to enable you to hear God's still, small voice?
2. Like Elijah, we can sometimes feel isolated, discouraged, and full of self-pity. At such times, what do we need to do to get out of the pit that engulfs us?

THE BOOK OF 2 Kings

Chapters 1–4

1. As Elisha desired a double portion of the Spirit that dwelt in Elijah, do you also want to have *all* the Holy Spirit desires to give you? Or are you content to stay where you are spiritually? Do you believe He wants you to have more?
2. Just as the widow's supply of oil continued flowing, make a list of some of the times when God has blessed you in unmistakable ways.

Chapters 5–7

1. As God used the little Jewish slave girl, share a time when a simple act of kindness to you (or someone else) made a significant difference.
2. Reflect on the statement that God often asks us to take a step of faith before He moves in our lives.
3. Is there an issue in your life where you need Christ's eyes to see it as He does?

Chapters 8–10

1. As these chapters reveal, sin (or even partial obedience to God) can end in chaos, destruction, or death. How do you see this played out in your own life experience?

Chapters 11–13

1. In the account of the repairing of the house of God, He clearly blesses honesty and integrity. How have you experienced this as a reality in your own life?

2. A great many people in our day have turned their backs on God. Do you believe our country faces serious consequences for this lack of honouring God?

Chapters 14–16

1. What "high places" (i.e. unconfessed sin and rebellion) might exist in the Church today, and in our personal lives? How can we deal with them?
2. Take some time to write down any areas of your life where you need to repent and receive Christ's forgiveness.

Chapters 17–19

1. In what ways (attitudes or actions) might we be called upon to go against the flow and stand up for righteousness in the face of opposition and rejection?
2. How can you, like Hezekiah, seek wisdom in the difficult grey areas of your life?

Chapters 20–25

1. God holds us accountable for everything He has given us. What legacy will you pass on to the next generation?
2. Part of our role as the Body of Christ is to pray for, encourage, and sometimes correct one another. Are you accountable to even one Christian brother or sister? If not, why?

THE BOOK OF *Romans*

Chapters 1–2

1. Reflect on Romans 1:11–12, as it could relate to those you love and care about. Think of ways you can offer encouragement and affirmation to another person today.
2. Christ's love and salvation is a gift offered us to which we can say, "No." Choosing ungodly living while being aware of God's way ultimately leads to misery and destruction. Do you agree? Why or why not?

Chapters 3–4

1. Trusting God's ways and His character is never easy when lived out in human relationships such as marriage. Why is forgiveness and repentance so basic to every deeper relationship?
2. Do you actively encourage and build up others around you? Why is loving unconditionally so difficult?
3. Abraham's amazing faith and obedience to God was born out of his intimacy with Him. What can we learn from the life of Abraham?

Chapters 5–6

1. Reflect on Romans 5:1. If our relationship with Christ is transparent and genuine, His gift to us is peace and His indwelling presence, regardless of circumstances. Which of your circumstances need more of His peace and presence?
2. Meditate on Romans 5:1–5. How does one get to that place of rejoicing in suffering?

3. Every believer struggles with at least one persistent sinful attitude or behaviour. What is yours? Are you willing to let the Saviour enable you to become an overcomer? What blocks you from saying "yes"?

Chapters 7–8

1. These chapters well describe the ongoing battle with sin in the believer's life. Have you truly experienced the amazing unconditional love of Jesus? If not, discuss this with someone who will pray with you.
2. What fills your mind? Just as having a healthy diet is good for you, how can the feeding of your mind be healthy and balanced?
3. In gratitude, reflect on the four spiritual realities the author lists at the end of this section. Are they real to you?

Chapters 9–10

1. These chapters clearly set out the distinction between law and grace. Being in right relationship with Jesus Christ will be reflected in what we do, and bring true salvation. Obeying the law only brings pain, defeat, and dissatisfaction. Do you agree?
2. How can you increase your times with God?
3. How can negative personal inner vows become a bondage and denial of what Jesus longs to do and be in our lives? (For example, saying, "I'm never good enough.")

Chapters 11–12

1. Romans 11 is a clear statement of God's yearning for all people—Jews and Gentiles alike—to come into personal intimacy with Him. How would you explain this passage to a new believer?
2. Romans 12 is an astounding summary of the gospel message—being in right relationship with God (12:1), with ourselves (1:2–3), with the Body of Christ (1:4–8), and with the world around us (1:9–21). Reflect on where you stand in terms of these four kinds of relationships.

Chapters 13–14

1. In our independent, individualistic culture, why is submission to authority so difficult for us?
2. Reflect on Romans 13:9–10. In what specific ways will you love your neighbour today? Next week? Ask the Lord for His thoughts on this!

3. What comes to mind as you reflect on Romans 14:13?

Chapters 15–16

1. Ask the Lord to show you where self-centredness may be blinding you to God's will for your life.
2. Thinking of Romans 15:15, how could you best be a reconciler and bring unity in stressful or broken relationships?
3. Joy and peace of mind is God's promised spiritual birthright to all believers. Is anything robbing you from overflowing with hope?

THE BOOK OF 1 Chronicles

Chapters 1–10

1. Our lives are comprised of ongoing choices which ultimately make us the people we are. How would you define a "successful" person?
2. What does it mean to do what is right in the sight of the Lord? Does your present-day life reflect that?

Chapters 11–13

1. Reflect on the amazing miracle of Israel being reborn in 1948, after almost two thousand years of the Jewish people being dispersed throughout the world. What do you believe is God's intent in this reality?
2. How would you describe your personal relationship with God? What could be changed or improved in your commitment?

Chapters 14–16

1. Are you content with your place in life right now? What do you believe God might be saying to you about it?
2. Do you make adequate time daily to simply worship God and in gratitude praise Him for who He is and what He is doing in your life? List some ways you could increase this time.

Chapters 17–22

1. David continued to fight battles throughout most of his reign, yet he walked in faithful victory. What are the enemies you face in your life? In our culture? Are you actively seeking to defeat them?

Chapters 23–29

1. Just as we need to eat well every day to maintain good health, we need to spend time with the Lord if we are to sustain an intimate relationship with Him. Are your quiet times life-giving or have they become mechanical?
2. Spend some time reflecting, writing, and /or discussing David's instructions to Solomon in 1 Chronicles 28:9.

THE BOOK OF 2 Chronicles

Chapters 1–7

1. How would you define wisdom? Solomon asked for it ahead of wealth, honour, long life, and the death of his enemies (3 Chronicles 1:10–12). Share some times when you sought wisdom from the Lord.
2. As God clearly chose Solomon to be king and to build the temple, what do you believe God has chosen for you to be and do in this life?
3. *"The glory of the Lord filled the temple of God"* (2 Chronicles 5:14). Describe one of the most significant and powerful times of worship you have experienced.

Chapters 8–13

1. Reflect on your understanding of suffering. Are there positive values that can emerge from suffering?
2. What does it mean to you to be a good steward of the blessings that are yours in Christ Jesus? Is there a need for some changes in how you live your life?

Chapters 14–16

1. Reflect on the promise in 2 Chronicles 15:2. Why is it so easy to get side-tracked from the priority of wanting God first, rather than an answer to our prayers?
2. Reflect on King Asa's behaviour described in 2 Chronicles 16:12. How can difficult circumstances sometimes turn us against God? What are the lies in our thinking?

Chapters 17–20

1. Meditate on 2 Chronicles 20:12–17. What are the truths and promises given here regarding spiritual battle?
2. Why is praising God the most potent weapon we possess in facing spiritual darkness? Have you experienced this?

Chapters 21–26

1. Consider the statements the author makes regarding our influence on others and their influence on us. What is to be learned from this?
2. Read 2 Chronicles 25:27. What steps can we take to assure that pride does not creep in and overtake our lives?

Chapters 27–30

1. Reflect on King Hezekiah's letter to Israel and Judah in 2 Chronicles 30:6–9. Thank the Lord for His mercy, compassion, and ever-open arms to receive us when we turn to Him.
2. Forgiveness is incomplete if we do not fully repent before Christ of our own sinful reactions towards those who hurt us. Ask Him to show you your heart, and to clean out any bitterness, pride, anger, or hatred that may still linger.

Chapters 31–36

1. Pride and self-sufficiency (as was the case with Hezekiah) can subtly distance us from God. What steps can we take to assure that we remain clean and transparent before Him?
2. The Church in North America has been described as being asleep in the light. What can we, as individuals and as a fellowship of believers, do to fight complacency?

THE BOOK OF
1 Corinthians

Chapters 1–3

1. Have you ever asked God for His wisdom? Are you a teachable person? What is involved in being teachable?
2. Do you expect God to work through your life? Reflect on 1 Corinthians 3:6. Planting and watering are very specific actions. Are you consciously planting seed and nurturing others? What may this involve for you?
3. Meditate on 1 Corinthians 3:16. Write down what this actually means to you.

Chapters 4–7

1. Respond to this statement: "Your actions speak so loudly that I cannot hear what you are saying."
2. Sexual permissiveness is rampant even within the Church today. Why do you believe God's rules regarding sexual activity are clearly restricted to traditional marriage? How might you explain this to someone else?

Chapters 8–10

1. Being judgmental and petty can easily invade every close relationship. How can you best overcome these annoying situations?
2. How does praying for and with someone make a difference in our outlook and responses?
3. Why is a meaningful daily time with the Lord so vital in maintaining a healthy, growing relationship with God?

Chapters 11–13

1. What spiritual truths are taught in 1 Corinthians 11:17–34? What does sharing in the Lord's Supper really mean to you?
2. What do you believe are your spiritual gifts? How can you know for sure and keep growing?
3. Reflect upon and memorize 1 Corinthians 13:4–8. Are there difficult, hard to love people in your life? How do these verses suggest ways you can overcome your negative attitudes and reactions?

Chapters 14–16

1. Think about 1 Corinthians 14:1. Are you always open and teachable as to what God wants to reveal to you and give you? What might stop you?
2. Prophesy can often be *forthtelling* (i.e. open and direct). Are you ready and willing to "speak up," even in intimidating situations, or do you generally just keep quiet?
3. Speak out loud and claim the promises in 1 Corinthians 15:57–58. Discuss ways you can become an overcomer and walk in victory.
4. 1 Corinthians 16:13–14 is a relevant, powerful reminder to keep in the forefront of your mind! Write it on a card in your Bible and think about it daily.

THE BOOK OF

2 Corinthians

Chapters 1–3

1. With 2 Corinthians 1:3–4 in mind, what have been the most valuable lessons you have learned during times of struggle and trouble?
2. Reflect on 2 Corinthians 3:17. What does it mean to you?
3. Are there questions or facets of the doctrine and ministry of the Holy Spirit that make you uncomfortable or confused?

Chapters 4–6

1. Ask the Lord to reveal to you the reason for the blindness or veil over the minds of unbelievers close to you. Pray for them accordingly.
2. 2 Corinthians 4:6–10, 16 offers us a powerful affirmation of faith. Personalize it as a prayer declaration using your own name.
3. Reflect on 2 Corinthians 5:17. Salvation is an ongoing process of becoming more like our Saviour, Jesus. What still remains of the "old" in your life?

Chapters 7–9

1. The author speaks of the necessity of spending time every day with God for confession and cleansing. In what ways can you keep your quiet time from becoming a rote and mechanical exercise?
2. Reflect on 2 Corinthians 9:6. Tithing of income is never mentioned in the New Testament. Given your present circumstances, what percentage of your time, your money, your home, your spiritual gifts are you willing to sow into Kingdom ministry?

3. Do you agree with the statement "You can't outgive God"? Why or why not?

Chapters 10–13

1. Read 2 Corinthians 10:3–6. How can you grow and mature in coping with the inner spiritual battle we all face? Do you have a trusted friend who could be your spiritual partner?
2. The spiritual battle begins in the mind. Satan is described as a liar and deceiver. Consider what lies or deceptions are part of your inner self-talk.
3. Reflect on 2 Corinthians 12:9. Let the Lord speak to you, and enjoy His incredible love for you.

THE BOOK OF
Ezra

Chapters 1–6

1. How attached are you to the comfortable lifestyle you now have? If God laid it on your heart, would you be willing to leave your home, family, or job to be involved in a difficult, costly challenge?
2. Reflect on those circumstances where you have clearly seen God at work in the lives of others, even non-believers.

Chapters 7–11

1. What do you know and believe about fasting? How can it be helpful in spiritual growth and maturity?
2. God commanded the people of Israel not to intermarry. What grey areas in your life do you need to examine?

THE BOOK OF
Nehemiah

Chapters 1–7

1. Are the Jewish people truly chosen by God to be a unique and separate people group? Reflect on the amazing reality that they are now a vibrant nation in their own homeland.
2. Reflect on Nehemiah's prayer in Chapter 1. Note how he *"mourned and fasted and prayed before the God of heaven"* (Nehemiah 1:4). He models something very significant here. Is this our response in times of crisis and loss?
3. In the building of the wall, each family took responsibility for their share of the work. How would the Church be different if each person or family took responsibility, using their gifts and doing their share of the ministry?
4. Do people see the hand of God in what you are doing—or what your church is doing?

Chapters 8–13

1. Look at Nehemiah 8:1–8. The people stood for hours to receive instruction from the Word of God. Do we revere and hunger after the Word of God in our lives? What can you do to instill that hunger in yourself and the people around you?
2. Nehemiah 13 describes how the people of Israel slid back into sinful behaviour patterns. In what areas of your life are you too slack, tolerant, or even disobedient in following God's rules for holy living?
3. Read Nehemiah 8:10 again. It concludes with: *"Do not grieve, for the joy of the Lord is your strength."* What does this verse mean?

THE BOOK OF *Esther*

1. If possible, read this book in one sitting. What responses do you have to this amazing saga?
2. What do you think enabled Esther to stand alone, prepared to face the possibility of death?
3. What are some of the truths to be learned from this lesson in history?
4. If at times there are circumstances that challenge you to stand up for what is right, even at great personal cost, are you ready? How can you prepare yourself—mentally, emotionally, and spiritually—to speak out at such a time as this?

THE BOOK OF
Galatians

Chapters 1–3

1. Reflect on Galatians 1:10. Are there areas in your life where it is easier to fit in by being a people pleaser, not speaking about your genuine convictions?
2. How would you paraphrase or explain what Paul means in Galatians 2:20? Is this your own commitment?
3. What thoughts come to mind as you reflect on Galatians 3:28?

Chapters 4–6

1. As you read these chapters, consider how our personal preferences and personality can sometimes crowd out Christ's love in our lives. Offer up to Him your petty criticisms and judgmental attitudes.
2. Let the Lord speak to your heart as you consider Galatians 5:6 and 5:22. Is your faith in Jesus reflected by the way you love others?
3. Reflect on Galatians 6:7–10. Make a list of people in your inner circle whom God has given to you. Ask the Lord how you can bless and encourage each one.

THE BOOK OF *Ephesians*

Chapters 1–3

1. With Ephesians 1:17 in mind, ask the Lord to grant you a deeper discernment about what He wants to do in you and through your life.
2. How would you explain the "one new man" (Ephesians 2:15) to a new Christian?
3. Speak out the prayer in Ephesians 3:14–21, meditating on each idea. Make it your personal commitment.

Chapters 4–6

1. Think over Ephesians 4:1 and ask yourself if you truly believe and live your life as if God has given you a specific vocation or calling. Can you identify what it is?
2. What does it mean to you to *"be filled with the Spirit"*? (Ephesians 5:18)
3. In an attitude of prayer, read over Ephesians 4:29–32. Write down what you sense God is saying to you through these verses.
4. Reflect on Ephesians 6:10–19. The six pieces of armour represent the full reality of who Jesus is. He is our protection as we face the world, and we need to put on our armour daily and *"pray in the Spirit on all occasions with all kinds of prayers and requests"* (Ephesians 6:18).

THE BOOK OF *Job*

Chapters 1–3

1. In this remarkably challenging, yet totally relevant book, we are confronted with the realities of God. How, in your mind, do these realities interconnect?
2. Job's three friends, often viewed in a negative light, *did* in fact share deeply in his loss and misery for seven days without saying a word (Job 2:12–13). How might we view differently our response to those who are wounded and experiencing brokenness?
3. How does Satan use fear or loss to deceive us and get us off-track spiritually?

Chapters 4–7

1. Do we, in fact, reap what we sow? (Job 4:8) Why are we so easily blinded by this truth?
2. As you read these chapters, can you personally testify to God's comfort, peace, and healing in times of distress?
3. How do you respond to times when God seems so distant and life makes no sense?

Chapters 8–12

1. When we face tragedy and injustice, what are better questions to ask than "why?"

2. Do hard times, loss, and tragedy really make us stronger and more understanding? Can you think of an example? What have you learned from these experiences?
3. In light of the spiritual struggle reflected in this passage, think about this statement: "In some ways, it is just as difficult to understand and explain the good things, the endless blessings and beauty in life, as it is to explain the tragic, unjust, and deeply wounding experiences we face."

Chapters 13–17

1. In the midst of hard times, do you have it out with God, sharing your anger, sense of injustice, and disappointments with Him? If not, why? He can handle it!
2. Often, when facing chaos and grief, we allow resentment, self-pity, and despair to become reactive sin to the wound we have received. We distance ourselves from God, and our negative thinking draws us into the deceptive, false schemes of Satan. Discuss.
3. Why are gratitude and praise so vital during hard times? (See Philippians 4:4–8)

Chapters 18– 23

1. Often, in going through trials, our closest friends disappoint and abandon us. We all are guilty of this, many times unintentionally. However, at the point of our greatest weakness, vulnerability, and brokenness, the reality of God's love and presence is never more real—when we let go of the lies and judgments, wanting only Him (Job 22:21). Discuss or write down some times in your life when you were disappointed by others or were a disappointment to someone else.
2. Share what you have learned throughout your dark times and how you were able to climb out of the pit. Pray with/for one another.
3. Sometimes when words won't come in prayer, praying out loud the promises of God (like Job 19:25–27, 23:10) lift the intensity of the pain and fog.
4. Times of trial by fire leave us either bitter or better. Reflect and discuss.

Chapters 24–31

1. Circumstances don't defeat us, unless we let them. Reflect and discuss. Identify some steps a follower of Jesus can take to rise above the circumstances.

2. Discuss Job 28:28. How would you explain this verse to a young child? Why are there seemingly so few wise persons among us?

Chapters 32–37

1. In relationship (intimacy with God), we discover meaning, purpose, and gain understanding about life (Job 32:8). What have you learned from the Bible about how to develop such a relationship? Discuss.
2. Consider the utterly beyond-the-beyond greatness of our God and the universe itself. Consider, likewise, how that same God thinks and feels about you! Worship Him!

Chapters 38–42

1. It is a dangerous thing to argue with God. Only as we see ourselves—unworthy, vulnerable, weak—in light of who He is can we gain the right balance and perspective on the issues of life. Discuss what you think this means.
2. Right relationship with God and right living brings great blessing—not necessarily great prosperity, as some Christians would insist. Reflect and discuss.
3. What important lessons and insights have you discovered by reading Job?

THE BOOK OF *Psalms*

Chapters 1–5

1. Do you often pray for Canada? For Israel? For other countries? How do you stay informed? Make a list of needs to pray for around the world and pray for them every day.
2. Are there times when you stay still and quiet in the Lord's presence? (Psalm 4:4) How do you deal with anger?
3. How would you describe the joy of the Lord? (Psalm 5:11) How might His joy differ from happiness?

Chapters 6–10

1. Most people highly value integrity and open honesty. How can you discover and learn about God's opinion about your choices and actions? (Psalm 7:11)
2. How do you experience God's correction and disapproval of your wrong attitudes, words, and actions?
3. Reflect on Psalm 8:3–4. Write down your thoughts about this passage.

Chapters 11–15

1. Do you feel comforted or uneasy knowing God is observing every part of your life? (Psalm 11:4)
2. Are there times when you have taken a stand for justice or what is right, even at personal cost? Have you ever backed away and remained silent? How can one know for sure when to take action?
3. Is there some area in your life where you have been disobedient to God's

leading or truth, and thereby compromised your intimacy with Him? If so, what action can you take?

Chapters 16–20

1. Self-centredness is a dominant characteristic in our culture. How can Jesus change your perspective?
2. Why is praise and worship of God so essential for spiritual living?
3. Reflect on Psalm 19:14. In what ways do your talk and inner thoughts need to change?

Chapters 21–25

1. Reflect on Psalm 22:1–3. How do you respond to those times when God seems distant, when you feel isolated and forgotten?
2. Does praising the Lord restore and revitalize your relationship with Him?
3. Write down and share with someone the many ways that goodness and mercy have followed you throughout your life (Psalm 23:6).
4. Learning to listen for and hear God's voice is a spiritual discipline as well as an immense gift from Him (Psalm 24:4). Be silent for a few moments right now to practise this.

Chapters 26–30

1. Is practicing the presence of God a top priority in your relationship with Jesus or do your needs, problems, and complaints dominate your conversation with God?
2. How does one learn to *"wait for the Lord"*? (Psalm 27:14)
3. Reflect on Psalm 30:11–12. How can we help each other get to that place of joy?

Chapters 31–35

1. It is a decision to be glad and rejoice—or, in other words, happiness is a choice. Do you agree? Why or why not?
2. It is clinically proven that resentment and unforgiveness can be contributing factors to some diseases. Reflect on how the gospel message of repentance and forgiveness truly is good news.
3. What can you do to become aware of what God is doing throughout the world? List situations that you believe have changed because of prayer.

Chapters 36–40

1. As you read these chapters, reflect on the qualities of God that most impact your life.
2. Reflect on Psalm 37:4–8. Focus on the verbs—delight, commit, be still, etc. Apply these words to your present life.

Chapters 41–45

1. What we want to receive from the Lord, we must be prepared to give to others. Do you agree? How can this principle be applied to your life?
2. Reflect on some of your most meaningful experiences of the presence of God. What did you learn from each encounter?
3. Persecution of Christians is one of the biggest human rights issues in the world. Pray for fellow believers who are paying a high price for being followers of Jesus.

Chapters 46–50

1. Psalm 46:1–3 is both a declaration and unfailing promise of our God, yet we often forget these words, especially during hard times. How can these words help us grow stronger in our faith?
2. Reflect on Psalm 46:10. What might need to change in your present lifestyle to include times of solitude and quiet contemplation?

Chapters 51–55

1. Reflect on Psalm 51:6. Why do so many followers of Christ suppress deep wounds from their past, carrying a burden of shame and self-rejection? What can we do about it?
2. Rewrite Psalm 51:10 in your own words as a personal prayer to the Lord.
3. With Psalm 51:17 and Psalm 55:22 as a focus, write down the thoughts that come to you.

Chapters 56–60

1. Though our minds may know of God's abiding love and presence with us, at times we feel isolated and cut off from Him. What would you say to someone in this position?
2. Fear, anger, and shame can be enemies in our lives. How does one find refuge in God at such times? (Psalm 57:1)

Chapters 61–65

1. Reflect on Psalm 62:5–8. Do you ever pour out your heart before God? Write down your inner struggles and share them with someone you trust.
2. In your quiet times and in public worship, do you consciously seek Christ's presence? What distracts you or blurs your focus?
3. Accepting the unconditional, complete forgiveness of our sin is an amazing, divine interaction between us and God. Why is it often difficult to receive His grace and fully forgive ourselves? (Psalm 65:3)

Chapters 66–70

1. Do you struggle with a besetting sin like bitterness, pride, or unforgiveness? If so, what is the lie you are buying into?
2. Reflecting on Psalm 68:5, how has the Lord met you during times of trauma and loss?
3. What is your response to the tragic, inexplicable events of this life? What attitude of mind, heart, and spirit helps to keep you from giving up your faith in God?

Chapters 71–75

1. Scripture paints many word pictures to describe God (Psalm 71:3). Write down some other descriptive terms—such as "shepherd" and "anchor." Which speak most powerfully to you? Why?
2. Reflect on Psalm 71:15–18. Do you ever actually speak to others about God's work and ministry in your life? Why or why not?
3. These chapters focus on praising, honouring, and glorifying God. It might be useful to ask yourself how much of your time with God is spent focussing on Him, and how much is spent focussing on your own needs, pains, and anxieties.

Chapters 76–80

1. Each generation of Christian believers is called to teach and live out by example the truth of God's salvation through Jesus. Are you consciously and intentionally passing on the reality of faith in Jesus Christ?
2. In what specific ways are you called to represent Jesus in your daily routine? Are there any places you need to change or re-evaluate your lifestyle?

Chapters 81–85

1. Are you growing in your spiritual gifts? In what way is sharing the grace of Jesus a part of your daily life? Is this awareness reflected in your prayer life?
2. How do you understand the role God has always had in mind for the Jewish people?
3. How do you account for the hatred and anti-Semitism in our world today?
4. Reflect upon Psalm 84:2.

Chapters 86–89

1. What new insights have you learned of the way of the Lord in the past year? Five years?
2. Most followers of Jesus experience times of spiritual dryness and feelings of separation from God's Spirit. How do you understand and get through such times? (Psalm 88:14)
3. What is the significance of Jerusalem in scripture and why is it so special to the Father's heart?

Chapters 90–95

1. Is God a valued, comfortable presence for you? Reflect on how the qualities of an ideal home and family are meant to be comparable to our experience with God.
2. Reflect on Psalm 90:12. How would you explain this verse to a ten-year-old?
3. Read Psalm 91 again. Note the incredible promises God makes to us as we seek Him first in our lives.

Chapters 96–100

1. Praising and worshipping God become deeper and richer the more we do it. Try it for a week and write down your discoveries—or questions.
2. Write down how you think God sees you personally (Psalm 98:9). Sometimes we ignore, deny, or repress God's unconditional love, justice, and righteousness.

Chapters 101–105

1. Spend time with Psalm 103 and make a list of the blessings of God in your life. Meditate with a prayer of gratitude for each blessing.
2. Consider prayerfully how you can express God's love to bless each person and circumstance He has given you.

Chapters 106–110

1. As you reflect on these chapters, consider that God's unchangeable promise to every believer who follows in His way is peace and joy, regardless of circumstance. Is this a present reality for you?
2. Ask the Lord to show you how to pray for our country's past failures, present problems, and future decisions. Make this a part of your quiet time with the Lord.

Chapters 111–115

1. Consider how Psalm 111:10 relates to you personally. In what areas of your life do you need a deeper understanding and more of God's power?
2. Think about how you use your time each day. Also consider your money and your home. Ask the Lord for His perspective on each aspect of your life.
3. How can you become more aware and proactive in being good stewards of God's creation?

Chapters 116–120

1. Take time to meditate on Psalm 116:1–2, especially if you have a nagging question or specific issue in your life.
2. Read the rest of this psalm, jotting down insights into God's character and His relationship with us.
3. Make a practice of praying scripture out loud.

Chapters 121–125

1. Meditate on Psalm 121:7–8, thinking back on your life with gratitude for God's goodness and provision. Then look to the future to capture His vision and desire for you. Write down your thoughts.
2. Why do you believe the Lord instructs us to pray for the peace of Jerusalem? (Psalm 122:6) Do you believe the Church should be

concerned about what goes on in the state of Israel today? Why or why not?

3. With these chapters in mind, write out a list of your core convictions and beliefs about God. Be aware of areas of unbelief, or doubts, and talk to the Lord about them.

Chapters 126—130

1. The author suggests that we sometimes restrict God to certain parts of our lives and don't allow Him into other areas. Do you agree? Can you give an example?
2. As you go about your daily schedule this week, focus on the relationships, activities, and material blessings that surround you. Offer prayers of gratitude to the Lord.
3. Reflect on Psalm 130:7 and God's unfailing love. Is there a memory or a wound in your past where you felt disappointed or let down by God? If yes, then seek out a mature fellow believer and pray together for a resolution of that pain or loss.

Chapters 131–136

1. Meditate on Psalm 131:2. How can you cultivate a quiet, restful heart?
2. Consider Psalm 133:1. The entire message of the Bible is about reconciliation in all our relationships—with God, with ourselves, with the Church, and with all the created order. Is there any resentment or bitterness in your past or present? What can you do about it?

Chapters 137–140

1. Reflect again on the unique phenomenon of the Jewish people being scattered throughout the world for almost two thousand years, yet not losing their ethnic and spiritual identity. Why do you think that is?
2. Psalm 139:23–24 is a marvellous, practical prayer that is helpful every day of our lives. Allow God to probe deeply into each part of your life and personality. Share this with a trusted friend.

Chapters 141–145

1. In order to hear God, we have to be open to making changes in our attitudes. Why is that hard to do?

2. Meditate on Psalm 141:3. Our words can build up or tear down, deeply wounding the people in our lives. What positive initiatives are you willing to take to communicate healing and encouragement to others?
3. David was dealing with very real physical enemies in this passage. Our enemies, however, are often within us—fear, secrecy, low self-esteem, and so on. What enemies do you face?

Chapters 146–150

1. Psalm 146:2 is a statement of conviction. An outlook of praise and gratitude to God is perhaps the most important spiritual discipline to which we can be committed. Make a list of five things for which you have never thanked God before.
2. Though we live in an ever-changing, often tragic, broken world, God's love and truth are unfailing and trustworthy. Find verses in this passage that bear out this reality.
3. Reflect on Psalm 147:11. Note how our Father God takes pleasure and delight in us when our hearts and minds are focussed on Him.

THE BOOK OF *Philippians*

Chapters 1–2

1. As you read the first chapter, ask the Lord that you, like Paul, could always see past the struggles and trials of the day, allowing God to use your life according to His purpose and plan (Philippians 1:6).
2. Do you view yourself as a servant of Jesus Christ, a servant who obeys the Master and fulfills His wishes? (Philippians 1:29)
3. What does it mean to work out your salvation with fear and trembling? Think of some examples.

Chapters 3–4

1. Reflect on Philippians 3:13–14. Is your purpose in life the same as God's purpose for you in this season of your life? If you're unsure about this, ask the Lord about it. What are you passionate about?
2. Meditate on the familiar, powerful, imperative words in Philippians 4:4–9. Apply these to your present life. We become the product of our thinking (Proverbs 27:19).

THE BOOK OF *Proverbs*

Chapters 1–5

1. Solomon asked the Lord for the gift of wisdom. How would you define wisdom? Check out James 3:13–18.
2. Reflect on Proverbs 2:3–6. Where in your life do you lack understanding? In which areas is the right choice difficult and unclear? Take some time in solitude to seek God's opinion.
3. Reflect on Proverbs 3:5–7. Ask the Lord to show you His heart for you in all your ways. Write down what you believe He is saying to you.

Chapters 6–10

1. Reflect on each phrase of Proverbs 6:16–19. Do you have any unfinished business in these areas? What are you prepared to do about it?
2. As you reflect on Proverbs 6:20–21, what do you most value about your growing up years? What values would you most desire to instill in the hearts and minds of the next generation?
3. How would you explain Proverbs 8:13 to a ten-year-old child?

Chapters 11–15

1. How would you measure your life in terms of the absolute values of honesty, purity, selflessness, and love? Use the verses the author uses from Proverbs 11 to stimulate your thinking.
2. If you committed yourself to living with absolute integrity, what attitudes and behaviours would you need to adjust and change?

Chapters 16–20

1. Reflect on Proverbs 16:2–3. To what extent do you allow the Lord to shape your motives and lifestyle choices?
2. Consider Proverbs 16:18. Think of some examples where pride leads to ruin and disaster. How can arrogance and judgmental pride creep into our attitudes and behaviour?
3. Reflect on Proverbs 17:22. How can one cultivate a cheerful, positive heart?

Chapters 21–25

1. How do you generally respond to correction, or positive criticism? Why?
2. In what areas of your life are you consciously seeking to grow and change? See Proverbs 23:12.
3. How can envy and jealousy rob you of joy and contentment?

Chapters 26–31

1. Reflect on Proverbs 26:20. What are the qualities of a peacemaker? Are you one?
2. Think about Proverbs 28:13.
3. Are you accountable—morally and spiritually—to anyone?
4. With Proverbs 31 as a backdrop, do you believe men are generally not held in respect in our culture? Why or why not?

THE BOOK OF *Ecclesiastes*

Chapters 1–6

1. Reflect on Ecclesiastes 1:3. What is your passion? What makes even the tough times, the drudgery, worthwhile?
2. Ecclesiastes 2:26 gives us an incredible promise. How would you define wisdom, knowledge, and happiness? Are you experiencing this? Why or why not?
3. Consider Ecclesiastes 5:10. How can you bring a balance between the need for money and being content with what you have?

Chapters 7–12

1. Think about Ecclesiastes 7:14. Do you withdraw from intimacy with God during bad times? Or during the good times? What do you need to readjust and learn?

THE BOOK OF *Colossians*

Chapters 1–2

1. Pray for those who are closest to you and who God has given you to love and encourage, using the five steps the author highlights from Colossians 1:3–11.
2. Apply the instruction found in Colossians 2:6–7 to your life in specific ways. Why is gratitude so important in our spiritual maturation?

Chapters 3–4

1. Meditate on Colossians 3:12–15. In prayer and in action, as the Holy Spirit guides you, respond to these verses. Meditate on them every day for a week.
2. As you think about Colossians 3:23, ask yourself: "Am I wholehearted, enthusiastic, and joyful in my work, in my relationships, and in giving back to God?
3. Jot down the things that come to mind as you reflect on Colossians 4:2

THE SONG OF *Songs*

1. Marriage for Christian believers is meant to be a covenant relationship. What is the difference between a covenant and a contract?
2. The Church, Jesus' followers, is referred to as the Bride of Christ in several places in scripture. In practical terms, what does this mean to you?

THE BOOK OF *Isaiah*

Chapter 1

1. Reflect on Isaiah 1:5. Are there areas of your life where you are rebellious against what you know to be the clear teaching of scripture?
2. Are some of your spiritual activities just going through the motions without engaging your heart or your will? How might you make the teaching of the Bible more relevant in your life?

Chapters 2–5

1. As you read these chapters, how do you explain why so much world attention is focused on the tiny nation of Israel?
2. It is the quality of life we live that counts. Do you agree? Do your attitudes and lifestyle reflect a positive or negative quality to others? What kind of fruit is your life producing?

Chapters 6–9

1. The glory of God is simply His presence. How can you experience His presence in your life?
2. Reflect on Isaiah 6:8. Are you consciously available to God in your daily routine? Do you think you are more often representing Him positively or negative?
3. Consciously consider the blessings or benefits of following Jesus Christ as Lord of your life. What results from disobedience?

Chapters 10–13

1. The Bible teaches, and history bears out, that selfishness, abuse of power, and evil always destroys. What areas of your life (attitudes, behaviours, etc.) need to be put right?
2. Reflect on Isaiah 11:1–2. These characteristics describing God's Spirit are all available to us as we seek to become more like Him.
3. Consider Isaiah 11:12. The miraculous rebirth of Israel in 1948 would seem to be predicted in this verse. What do you understand by this?

Chapters 14–17

1. What does it mean to you to make Jesus Christ the Lord of your life?
2. List the advantages and difficulty of having a quiet time of prayer and study of God's Word each day. Like any other discipline, this is a skill that deepens and becomes richer as we practice it.

Chapters 18–22

1. God's Spirit of love and truth enables us to have the willpower to overcome any sinful habit. What are you prepared to leave behind and hand over to the Lord Jesus Christ?
2. Anti-Semitism in an enlightened, rational world would seem to be irrational and nonsensical. How do you explain its existence today?

Chapters 23–26

1. Few of us like to admit that we are arrogant and egocentric, yet it is central to our humanity. How can one become more aware of and avoid the subtleties of pride and self-centredness?
2. Praise and gratitude eliminate self-pity and depression. Reflect and practise the declarations of Isaiah 25:1,8–9. What do you experience?
3. Isaiah 26:3 is a wonderful promise of God. It is the birthright of every believer. Explain the promises in your own words.

Chapters 27–30

1. These chapters bear a sobering reality. Discuss or write down what this means for your life today.
2. Note the numerous promises of God in these chapters. Claim those that speak to you most personally and list them to keep in front of you.

3. Tell about those times when the Lord has clearly guided your thoughts and choices. Continue to seek to hear His voice in everyday life.

Chapters 31–35

1. Reflect on the truth of the promises found in Isaiah 32:17. Tell of a time when you have walked in disobedience and experienced the consequences.
2. Think of those you know without the Saviour in their lives. Ask the Lord how you might reflect His love and truth to them.
3. Allowing Jesus to be the Lord in every part of our lives is a lifelong process of growth. Why do we resist Him so often?

Chapters 36–40

1. Sometimes we are slow to learn the lesson found in Isaiah 37:14. Practise taking every temptation and trial in your daily routine and seeking God in it.
2. Reflect on the incredible truths found in Isaiah 40:38–41. Have you ever realized that the greatest sense of God's presence and power can be at those times when we are barely able to stand and take the next step? Discuss times when you have experienced this.

Chapters 41–43

1. These chapters repeatedly affirm that God is faithful to His promises and can be trusted. Share with someone how the Lord has comforted, strengthened, and saved you in dark, overwhelming times.
2. Write down the most meaningful verses to you from this passage.

Chapters 44–47

1. Ask God to show you how to pray specifically for each person closest to you?
2. God's peace and joy are often experienced at those times of deepest struggle. Do you believe this is true? How does that affect your daily life?

Chapters 48–51

1. Isaiah repeatedly refers to the new things God is doing. What new awareness, insight, or answer to prayer have you experienced recently?

2. Keeping on the straight path is not always easy. Is there a fellow believer to whom you are accountable, and with whom you can be fully transparent?
3. Tell of a time you have experienced God's promise not to forget you?

Chapters 52–56

1. Reflect on Isaiah 55:6. Do you truly desire to receive *all* that God wants to give you? Are there places where you are unwilling to yield to Him, and avoid His promptings?
2. Describe how God's Word is like seed in soil, producing a harvest. Do you know and can you identify your purpose in this world?
3. Reflect on Isaiah 55:11–12. What does this mean to you?

Chapters 57–60

1. Reflect on Isaiah 57:15. How can one cultivate and maintain a humble, contrite spirit?
2. How might Isaiah 58:6–7 be applied to you where you live today? What is the Holy Spirit prompting you to do? Test the Lord and see that His promises become your reality (Isaiah 58:10).

Chapters 61–66

1. Jesus quoted Isaiah 61:1–3 as His job description for His time here on earth. Should it be our job description as His followers? Who are the poor, the broken-hearted, and the captives in your world?
2. Isaiah 61–62 clearly is God's prophetic proclamation about His chosen people, the Jews. How do you think followers of Jesus Christ should identify or relate to Jewish people today? Why do you think this is largely ignored by so many in the Church?
3. Memorize some of your favourite verses from Isaiah. Continue to meditate on them and apply them to your life.

THE BOOK OF

1 Thessalonians

Chapters 1–3

1. Reflect on 1 Thessalonians 2:4. God sees and knows our hearts. Are there places in your life where ego, self-defence, or the need to be affirmed distort and cloud your motives in serving God and others?
2. Meditate on 1 Thessalonians 3:12. Is your love for the people in your life active and growing, or is it sluggish or dormant? One way to determine this is to examine and evaluate your prayer life.

Chapters 4–5

1. Spending uncluttered, open times with the Lord is often a difficult spiritual discipline. Does busyness, overcommitment, or preoccupation with daily issues block your growing intimacy with Jesus? Write about the times during your day when you could meet with Jesus.
2. If Jesus were to unexpectedly come to your home today, would you be ready to greet Him? Or are there things that would make you embarrassed and uncomfortable in His presence?
3. 1 Thessalonians 5:16–18 gives us a simple, uncomplicated instruction. Practise this teaching for a week and then take note of what you have learned and experienced.

THE BOOK OF

2 Thessalonians

Chapters 1–3

1. The threefold prayer request noted by the author deserves serious, sober contemplation. Keep a journal of thoughts and specific ideas the Lord brings to your mind in the next few days.
2. The words of 2 Thessalonians 2:16–17 are a familiar benediction in many churches. Benediction means to "speak good." Think of those who might be blessed and encouraged by a good word from you today.
3. How would you explain the "Lord of peace" to an unbeliever?

THE BOOK OF *Jeremiah*

Chapters 1–3

1. Read Jeremiah 1:5. Do you believe that all of Christ's followers have a specific call of God on their lives? What about you?
2. Every aspect of our Western culture is being infiltrated by secular humanism. What are the dangers in this approach? What does Scripture teach?
3. What negative, sinful attitudes and behaviours have you grown to accept in your life? How could you change these?

Chapters 4–7

1. With Jeremiah 4:1–2 as a backdrop, how would you explain genuine repentance, or turning back to God?
2. Why is it that so many people seem not to fear the consequences of greed, violence, wastefulness, and immorality?

Chapters 8–11

1. Reflect on Jeremiah 8:6 and the author's comments. Why do you think seeking God's direction is resisted by so many people?
2. Consider Jeremiah 8:11. How would you describe the peace of God? What is required on our part to experience His peace?
3. The expression "the fear of the Lord" is used many times in Scripture (see Proverbs). What does this involve for the believer?

Chapters 12–16

1. Reflect on Jeremiah 12:3. Why is the reality of God knowing our innermost beings a comfort or "intolerable burden," as the author puts it?
2. Reflect on the immensity of the prophecy in Jeremiah 16:14–16. What do you believe the response of the Church and individual believers should be to Israel?

Chapters 17–21

1. Reflect on Jeremiah 17:7–8. How would this beautiful promise be experienced and interpreted in one's personal life? Do you believe it?
2. Why is it that we can often live so comfortably with sin in our lives? See Jeremiah 17:9–10. How might this double-minded, false self be part of the strategy of Satan, who is described as a liar and deceiver?
3. Consider Jeremiah 21:8 and compare with Deuteronomy 30:19–20. God does, indeed, grant each of us a choice throughout life—His way or our way!

Chapters 22–25

1. As stated before, learning to hear the voice of God is a skill that is learned as we go. How can you be sure that you have really heard God in a given situation?
2. Reflect on the warnings and conditions for receiving God's direction and empowerment in our lives. See Jeremiah 22:3–5. Are you in denial or avoiding dealing with any issues from your past?

Chapters 26–29

1. Jeremiah felt very much alone in his mission as a prophet to Israel. How do you work through those times when you feel lonely and isolated from everyone around you?
2. Are you actively involved, alone or with others, in speaking out against the evils and brokenness in our communities? Do you believe God gives us specific assignments to accomplish for Him?
3. Memorize and reflect on the wonderful promises in Jeremiah 29:11–14. Think about these promises in your past and what they may mean in your future. Record these thoughts in your journal.

Chapters 30–33

1. Think over Jeremiah 30:2. Record your prayers and the answers, then reread them as an encouragement in hard times.
2. Reflect on Jeremiah 31:3. Spend some time allowing the Lord to fully embrace you with His unconditional love.
3. Have you ever sought God for a seemingly impossible request? See Jeremiah 32:17. How do you understand those times when your petitions appear to be unanswered?

Chapters 34–38

1. There are so many voices clamouring for our attention. Many are not of themselves evil or wrong, but can distract us and steer us off-course. How can you maintain a balanced outlook and response to the demands and challenges coming your way?
2. Like Jeremiah, you may be asked to deliver an unwelcome, difficult message to someone. How can you best overcome passivity and timidity in facing hard challenges?

Chapters 39–45

1. Virtually everyone has some specific area of temptation to sin that continually lures them away from God. What can you do today to be free of sinful, destructive thought patterns and behaviours?
2. With Jeremiah 42:19 as a backdrop, how do you respond to people you care about deeply who choose to move into destructive patterns of behaviour?

Chapters 46–52

1. Reflect on Jeremiah 46:28. How would you respond to an agnostic who believes there can't be a God of justice given our broken, tragic world?
2. Evil, and opposing God, ultimately brings destruction and ruin, whether it's a nation or an individual. Do you agree? Can you think of some examples?
3. The author's last comment on leadership is profound. If you are in leadership, do you have ongoing prayer cover by trusted intercessors? Choose a few leaders to pray for regularly. Let them know you are praying and keep in touch to find out what their needs are.

THE BOOK OF *Lamentations*

Chapters 1–5

1. Make a list of some specific things you can do or pray for regarding our country, our city, or your family.
2. Lamentations 3:22–23 should be an ongoing song of praise and gratitude for each of us, even on the bad days. What and for whom are you specifically grateful for today?
3. Lamentations 3:40 is an appropriate ongoing reminder. Consider the verbs—examine, test, and return—as they apply to your life.

THE BOOK OF
1 Timothy

Chapters 1–3

1. Paul's letters to Timothy describe and encourage strong, Christ-centred leadership. Is there a potential Christian leader you can bless with your insights, time, and experience?
2. What ideas stand out for you in this passage? Why?
3. Consider 1 Timothy 3:5. Is your witness of Christ the same in your home as it is with your Christian circle of friends? Why or why not? What can you do to improve your witness at home?

Chapters 4–6

1. How would you evaluate your Christian influence on those people who are part of your everyday life?
2. How deeply do you care for others in your circle of relationships? Are you personally involved with others who may not be followers of Christ? If not, what changes could you make?
3. How do you explain to others and yourself our lifestyle of abundance and ease in North America, when so many in the world barely have enough to eat?

THE BOOK OF
2 Timothy

Chapters 1–4

1. Reflect on 2 Timothy 1:6–7. Do you intentionally consider your spiritual gifts and seek to deepen and grow in them? Verse 7 is a powerful promise we can claim. Write it out in your journal to read often.
2. What do you need to believe differently about yourself in order to become more obedient to the call of God on your life?

THE BOOK OF *Ezekiel*

Chapters 1–4

1. Do you have a sense of mission for being in the workplace/neighbourhood/church where you are now? (Ezekiel 2:3)
2. What are some of your struggles and fears in doing what you believe God has called you to do?
3. Practise listening for God's prompting voice. What do you think He is saying to you today?

Chapters 5–9

1. Like the Israelites of Ezekiel's day, we can easily absorb ideas and behaviours that are contrary to God's ways. What does it mean to be *in* the world but not *of* the world?
2. How do you understand and feel about the harsh consequences God sometimes allows us to receive for rebellious living?

Chapters 10–15

1. The prevailing message is that trust and obedience releases God's blessing and favour. Disobedience brings very negative, destructive results. How do you respond to God's angry response to the Israelites' rebellion?
2. Israel is sometimes referred to as "God's timepiece" since His eternal historic plans seem to revolve around the Jews. Consider the implications of the state of Israel in our day (Ezekiel 11:17).

Chapters 16–20

1. How is a covenant different from a contract? How should this influence the institution of marriage, especially for followers of Christ?
2. God's continual forgiveness whenever we repent is an amazing gift (Ezekiel 18:21–30). Why is repentance often a struggle for us?

Chapters 21–25

1. It is not circumstances that make or break us, but rather our attitude towards them and what we do with them. Discuss.
2. Scripture repeatedly asserts that God's judgment will come against those who oppose Israel, both individually and as nations (Ezekiel 25). Is this taught in your church? What can you do to bring this message to other believers?

Chapters 26–33

1. Reflect on Ezekiel 28:4. What creates pride in our hearts, our attitudes, and even our behaviour? Why is it such a subtle sin?
2. How can a follower of Jesus determine what is a healthy balance in relation to wealth and material things?
3. Reflect on Ezekiel 33. What can be learned in your life from Israel's ongoing fall into temptation and disobedience, even though the Lord repeatedly rescued them and proved His justice and mercy?

Chapters 34–36

1. Reflect on the beautiful description of God as a caring shepherd in Ezekiel 34:11–16. How can this picture become distorted in our minds?
2. With Ezekiel 36 as background, consider how God is working out His eternal plans for mankind through the Jewish people.
3. The promise of Ezekiel 36:26 is that we will receive a new heart and spirit. Is this the same as Jesus' offer of salvation for all who follow Him?

Chapters 37–39

1. Like Israel, all of us pass through seasons of dry, spiritual wilderness. How would you counsel a believer who is walking through such a time?
2. List the people and things for which you are specifically grateful today. Ask the Lord to reveal to you how best to pray for each person.

3. In light of this scripture (Ezekiel 37:21–22), how do you interpret present-day world events?

Chapters 40–48

1. Israel's rebellion is referred to often in these chapters. Might a verse like Ezekiel 44:6 be what God is saying to the Church in North America today?
2. If we are indeed living in the end times, as many believe, how should we be living and teaching differently?

THE BOOK OF *Daniel*

Chapters 1–5

1. Daniel, Shadrach, Meshach, and Abednego all faced certain death in staying true to honouring their God. When faced with a life-threatening challenge, how strong is your faith? How would you respond?
2. Have you ever fully trusted God, like Daniel, to give you special wisdom? (Daniel 2:28) How does a follower of Jesus develop faith like this?
3. Daniel 3:18 shows that the three men had total trust in God to protect them. Think of an example of someone who has prayed confidently for a miracle. What was the outcome?

Chapters 6–12

1. What is the nature of your prayer life? Is it growing as you walk with the Lord? What changes need to happen?
2. When unsure of where to begin or how to pray, gratitude is a good place to start. List some things you are grateful for in your situation right now.
3. Reflect on Daniel 10:12. Do you think this promise was only for Daniel? How does it impact on your life?
4. After expressing gratitude to God, what other kinds of prayers might bring His presence closer? Write these in your journal.

THE BOOKS OF

Titus & Philemon

1. How do you think the Church is viewed by non-believers in our country? List both positive and negative assessments.
2. Titus 3:1–2 is a major command of challenge to all of us. As followers of Jesus, how can we make our faith a full-time lifestyle, not just an add-on?
3. What can you do to build relationships and disciple individuals who may be very different from you in outlook and lifestyle?

THE BOOK OF *Hosea*

Chapters 1–5

1. In light of Hosea's message, how do you think God views our country? What would He say to us as a nation? As the Church?
2. Re-establishing trust after we have been betrayed is almost impossible apart from Christ's love and forgiveness at work within us. How have you responded in the past when someone has broken faith with you or let you down? What did you learn from the experience? (Hosea 3:1)
3. How do you think the Church, and individual Christians, may be in rebellion to God's laws in our culture? What could be the consequences for our independent attitudes and actions? How do these attitudes affect our children?

Chapters 6–14

1. How do you think God views your relationship with Him? Your lifestyle? What may need to change?
2. What is your response to God when you face times of tragedy, loss, or injustice? Do they make you bitter or better?
3. When do you seek to hear from God about the choices and decisions you make? Is listening to Him a hit-and-miss thing or is it a daily discipline?
4. Reflect on Hosea 14:1,4. Where have you truly experienced God's incredible love, acceptance, forgiveness, and healing in your life?

THE BOOK OF *Joel*

Chapters 1–3

1. The message of Joel is that catastrophe simply exposes the spiritual and moral reality that exists in a nation or culture. God punishes sinful behaviour. Do you believe that a nation that turns away from God cannot escape His judgment? Discuss.
2. Joel also gives us a beautiful picture of hope. Reflect on Joel 2:12–13. God's love allows us to say no to Him, but He is always ready to forgive when we are ready to truly repent.
3. Do you routinely keep informed and pray for all levels of authority and leaders in our communities, cities, provinces, and country? Begin to pray for God's Holy Spirit to be poured out upon "all flesh" in our country.

THE BOOK OF *Hebrews*

Chapters 1–4

1. Why do so many active followers of Jesus turn away from involvement in local congregations? What does this mean? See Hebrews 3:12.
2. When you pray, do you pray to Jesus as our priest? What does this actually mean to you? See Hebrews 2:17.
3. Reflect on Hebrews 4:12–13. Allow these words to challenge you on the power of your words—both positively and negatively.

Chapters 5–7

1. Reflect on Hebrews 5:14. How would you describe a mature Christian? Would you consider yourself a mature follower of Christ? Why or why not?
2. It would seem that at least some Christians in our culture are primarily interested in what the church can do for them—great worship, inspired preaching, and good programs—but they give little in return. What are your thoughts about this?
3. Hebrews 7 describes Jesus as our great high priest, and those of us who profess faith in Christ have a priestly role as well. How would you describe this role?

Chapters 8–13

1. Reflect on Hebrews 9:14. How would you explain the meaning of Jesus' sacrifice on the cross?

2. Consider Hebrews 10:23–25. Persevering in our faith, especially during difficult times, is not always easy. What are some ways to encourage others as part of your Christian walk?
3. Meditate on the teaching from Hebrews 11–12. Use a different Bible translation, if possible, to gain further insight.
4. Meditate on and pray aloud Hebrews 13:20–21 each day for a week. What comes to your mind as you reflect on it?

THE BOOK OF *Amos*

Chapters 1–9

1. Amos, like all the prophets, spoke out strongly against injustice and the abuse of power, especially when it was found among the religious leaders. Consider where the church may be unaware or turning a blind eye to injustice in your community. What can you do about it?
2. What do you feel is your particular calling in your community to the “hidden poor” (i.e. the disabled, the single parents, the lonely, and perhaps First Nations).
3. Is there any area of your life which you feel you have not totally given to God? Why not?

THE BOOK OF *Obadiah*

Chapter 1

1. After centuries of war and rivalry between Israel and Edom, Obadiah prophesies about a time to come when Edom will be ruled with justice and mercy and God's laws will be honoured and obeyed by Israel. What signs do you see in the world today that love and justice are still very much alive and that evil ultimately will self-destruct?

THE BOOK OF *Jonah*

Chapters 1–4

1. Think back to a time when God clearly gave you a task to do. Have there been times when you ignored God's voice? If so, what have you learned from those experiences?
2. How can you confirm or know for sure that God is speaking to you? List at least three ways.
3. All of us need a friend or two like Jonah—very human and down to earth. What is so appealing about the story of Jonah?

THE BOOK OF *James*

Chapters 1–3

1. Do you struggle with James 1:2–3? Why is it nevertheless a very important teaching? Think of some personal examples of this truth.
2. Make a list of the practical, powerful teaching in these chapters. What verses speak to you most directly? Why?

Chapters 4–5

1. Have you ever tested the teaching in James 4:7–8? What have you discovered?
2. There is great power in the teaching of James 5:16. Why do you think this is so important?
3. What are the most important lessons and insights you have discovered from this study of James?

THE BOOK OF
Micah

Chapters 1–7

1. The tone of the first part of Micah is like that of frustrated parents whose children will not listen and obey. It is directed towards Israel's leaders. God allows His people to self-destruct. What parallels do you see between Micah's time and our own?
2. Starting in Micah 4, he speaks about God giving the people new life. How do you view the return of Jesus Christ to earth?
3. What can you do to strengthen your connection with Israel and the Jewish people?
4. Meditate on Micah 6:8. How can you apply this powerful statement to your everyday life?

THE BOOK OF *Nahum*

Chapters 1–3

1. Whether it is an individual or a world power like Assyria and its capital city Nineveh, this spiritual principle holds true—good ultimately triumphs over evil! Do you agree? Think of some examples.
2. On a personal level, reflect on how Satan uses deception, distortion, and lies in the struggle to make sin appear attractive and desirable.

THE BOOK OF *Habakkuk*

Chapters 1–3

1. Times of silence in the presence of God are rare for a lot of Christ followers. Practise being quiet before the Lord as a spiritual discipline. Write down the thoughts that come to you. He may be speaking to you.
2. Reflect on Habakkuk 3:17–18. Giving God praise and thanksgiving is a decision, not always a feeling. Make your own list of negatives and hand them over to the Lord as a deliberate choice.

THE BOOK OF

1 Peter

Chapters 1–5

1. Reflect on 1 Peter 1:15–16. The word "holy" is derived from the concept of "wholeness." Does this help your understanding?
2. How might 1 Peter 4:8 be lived out in a daily, practical way?
3. Take some time to write out the anxieties you carry, then hand them over to the Lord.

THE BOOK OF

2 Peter

Chapters 1–3

1. As you meditate on 2 Peter 1:3, ask yourself, do you really believe that God desires to fulfill every part of your life, regardless of circumstances? (See John 10:10)
2. Consider 2 Peter 1:5–9. What can you do to grow deeper in your faith walk with Jesus every day?
3. Reflect on 2 Peter 2:19, which says that people are slaves to whatever masters them. Is there any habit or sin in your life that leaves you feeling defeated? Consider acting on James 5:16.

THE BOOK OF

Zephaniah

Chapters 1–3

1. Our human response to religion is often to want closeness with God, but this may exclude the kind of relationship we have with each other. Reflect on the way you treat people, especially those you do not like. Zephaniah says that *every* relationship is a reflection of our relationship with God. How does this statement challenge you?
2. What are you doing with long-held bitterness and unforgiveness? What patterns exist in how you deal with unhealthy relationships?
3. The prophets proclaim that the consequences of how we have related to God and to the people in our world will come together on Judgment Day. What is your understanding of Judgment Day?

THE BOOK OF *Haggai*

Chapters 1–2

1. Haggai's sole concern is that the place where God's people meet be honouring to Him. How does this translate into our culture?
2. Are you concerned primarily with your own needs, projects, and dreams, with the work of God trailing far behind in your thoughts and plans? What are your motives in giving?
3. Many Christians faithfully tithe their income, yet tithing is never mentioned in the New Testament. Why do you think this is so?

THE BOOKS OF

1 John, 2 John, 3 John

1. Reflect on 1 John 1:5–10, contrasting light and darkness in both spiritual and practical terms.
2. 1 John 2:9–11 makes it very clear that there is to be no place for unforgiveness and unreconciled relationships on our part as followers of Jesus. Ask the Lord to show you where areas of resentment, jealousy, or hardness of heart exist toward anyone.
3. Worship and thank God for the powerful affirmations of 1 John 3:1–3.
4. As you read and reflect on these letters of John, make a list of those teachings that challenge and bless you, acting on what the Lord places on your heart.

THE BOOK OF *Jude*

Chapters 1

1. Jude 20–23 carries sound advice for every day. Write this advice in your own words, as it relates to your life.
2. Use the benediction of Jude 24–25 as a frequent act of affirmation, praise, and worship of our God.

THE BOOK OF *Zechariah*

Chapters 1–7

1. What is your vision of God working His sovereign plans for our world? When have you felt that you were part of God's eternal purposes?
2. Reflect on Zechariah 4:6. Can you think of examples where God has done the seemingly impossible against all odds?

Chapters 8–14

1. Reflect on the three prophesies the author notes from this passage. How should we be preparing for the second coming of the Lord? Do you think we should be involved in specific activities toward this end?
2. Should we, as individual believers, in some way be intentionally connected with Jewish people? Why or why not?
3. What is your understanding of such bitter hatred or indifference against Israel by so many of the world's nations?

THE BOOK OF *Malachi*

Chapters 1–4

1. What have you discovered about God and yourself during difficult times of trial? How can a positive attitude make a crucial difference when times are tough?
2. Why do you think God gets crowded to the fringe of our lives during "normal" times?
3. How can unforgiveness rob us of the fullness and joy of God's presence?
4. Reflect on Malachi 3:10. Write a few sentences explaining what this means for you.

THE BOOK OF *Revelation*

Chapters 1–3

1. Seeking the help of the Holy Spirit, reflect on the messages to the seven churches (Revelation 2–3) and what they reveal about ourselves and the congregations of which we are a part. How can God use you to bring necessary changes to your fellowship?

Chapters 4–7

1. As you reflect on God's character as described in Revelation 4–5, spend time in silence, thanksgiving, and worship of our amazing God.
2. Meditate on the promises of hope found in Revelation 7:14–17 for comfort as we look to that future day. Explain how you understand these verses.

Chapters 8–11

1. If praying is a conversation with God, how can you make these times more meaningful and life-changing?
2. Revelation 8–9 speaks of trumpets ushering in a time of God's judgment. How do you picture this? What can you do today to prepare yourself for His return?
3. Amid the chaos and breakdown in our world, the Christian's hope and belief is that God ultimately will have the final word and His perfect will shall become a reality (Revelation 11:15). What does this mean to you?
4. The author speaks of the joy of the Lord, a gift to all believers, regardless of circumstance (Nehemiah 8:10). When have you experienced this?

Chapters 12–18

1. The description of the great tribulation is a three-and-a-half-year period of global suffering and despair. Such suffering is already happening today in many places in the world. How do you, as a Christian, respond to world poverty, disease, and injustice?
2. The hope, joy, and ever-present love of Jesus Christ keep us centred during even the worst of times. Is this your experience, or do anxiety, fear, and doubt crowd out His presence?
3. Examine again your personal relationship with Jesus. Is it hit-and-miss or is it an intentional daily interaction with the Lord and with His Word?

Chapters 19–20

1. What do you think Paul means by *"a sacrifice of praise"* in Hebrews 13:15?
2. Do you routinely ask the Lord to show you your heart from His perspective? What are the weak, vulnerable areas of your personality?

Chapters 20–21

1. What happens when a great leader becomes the dominant focus of a Christian's life, and how can you avoid this subtle trap?
2. Forgiveness and repentance through the power of Jesus' love form the core of the gospel message. Continue to make them a daily discipline in your spiritual walk.
3. What lessons or thoughts have been the most profound for you in reading all the way through the Bible?